COUNTIES
OF
TENNESSEE

By AUSTIN P. FOSTER, A.M.

Copyright, 1923
DEPARTMENT OF EDUCATION, DIVISION OF HISTORY
State of Tennessee

Reprinted for Clearfield Company, Inc.
by Genealogical Publishing Company Inc.
Baltimore, Maryland
1992

ISBN 0-8063-5061-X

INDEX

	Page		Page
Anderson County	5	Lake County	114
Bedford County	46	Lauderdale County	114
Benton County	101	Lawrence County	65
Bledsoe County	6	Lewis County	66
Blount County	6	Lincoln County	67
Bradley County	7	Loudon County	26
Campbell County	9	McMinn County	27
Cannon County	47	McNairy County	117
Carroll County	102	Macon County	68
Carter County	10	Madison County	115
Cheatham County	49	Marion County	28
Chester County	103	Marshall County	69
Claiborne County	11	Maury County	70
Clay County	50	Meigs County	29
Cocke County	12	Middle Tennessee	46
Coffee County	51	Monroe County	30
Chester County	103	Montgomery County	72
Crockett County	103	Moore County	75
Counties of Tennessee	4	Morgan County	32
Cumberland County	12	Obion County	118
Davidson County	52	Overton County	76
Decatur County	104	Perry County	77
DeKalb County	54	Pickett County	78
Dickson County	55	Polk County	33
Dyer County	105	Preface	3
East Tennessee	5	Putnam County	78
Fayette County	106	Rhea County	34
Fentress County	57	Roane County	35
Franklin County	58	Robertson County	80
Gibson County	107	Rutherford County	81
Giles County	59	Scott County	37
Grainger County	13	Sequatchie County	38
Greene County	14	Sevier County	39
Grundy County	61	Shelby County	119
Hamblin County	15	Smith County	83
Hamilton County	16	Stewart County	85
Hancock County	20	Sullivan County	40
Hardeman County	108	Sumner County	86
Hardin County	109	Tipton County	122
Hawkins County	21	Trousdale County	89
Haywood County	111	Unicoi County	42
Henderson County	112	Union County	43
Henry County	112	Van Buren County	90
Hickman County	62	Warren County	90
Houston County	63	Washington County	44
Humphreys County	64	Wayne County	92
Jackson County	65	Weakley County	123
Jefferson County	22	West Tennessee	101
Johnson County	23	White County	93
Knox County	24	Williamson County	94
		Wilson County	97

PREFACE

THIS book is not a history of Tennessee. It is, however, supplementary to the history of the state, for it gives historical and statistical facts, which are of general interest throughout the state and of particular interest to the people of the several counties. The purpose of the book is to enable the student, the investigator, and the casual searcher after information regarding our counties, to secure the salient points desired in a minimum of time. For this reason the information is given as laconically as is consistent with clearness. Moreover, this brevity is rendered necessary by the limitations of the book itself.

As only the most important historical events of the counties are given, those persons whose requirements demand a more detailed narrative of any county than is here given should consult the published history of that county, if it has appeared in book form. Unfortunately very few have so appeared. This fact is the more regrettable because every county in Tennessee is so rich in historical material that a book of good size could be written concerning it. For some, indeed, several volumes would be required for exhaustive exposition.

The statistics are from the United States census reports of 1920.

The preparation of this book has been rendered desirable, if not necessary, by the investigations instigated and prosecuted in the State Library with the assistance of the force of the Library and of the Division of History, in which investigations questions in regard to the counties of the state are constantly arising. Coupled with this condition are the numerous letters of inquiry asking for information concerning the counties which required research each time in order to answer. It is hoped, therefore, that this little book will meet a real want not heretofore supplied.

A. P. FOSTER.

COUNTIES OF TENNESSEE

POLITICALLY, Tennessee is divided into three Grand Divisions—East Tennessee, Middle Tennessee, and West Tennessee. The counties of East Tennessee are: Anderson, Bledsoe, Blount, Bradley, Campbell, Carter, Claiborne, Cocke, Cumberland, Grainger, Greene, Hamblen, Hamilton, Hancock, Hawkins, Jefferson, Johnson, Knox, Loudon, Marion, McMinn, Meigs, Monroe, Morgan, Polk, Rhea, Roane, Scott, Sequatchie, Sevier, Sullivan, Unicoi, Union, Washington—34.

The counties of Middle Tennessee are: Bedford, Cannon, Cheatham, Clay, Coffee, Davidson, DeKalb, Dickson, Fentress, Franklin, Giles, Grundy, Hickman, Houston, Humphreys, Jackson, Lawrence, Lewis, Lincoln, Macon, Marshall, Maury, Montgomery, Moore, Overton, Perry, Pickett, Putnam, Robertson, Rutherford, Smith, Stewart, Sumner, Trousdale, Van Buren, Warren, Wayne, White, Williamson, Wilson—40.

The counties of West Tennessee are: Benton, Carroll, Chester, Crockett, Decatur, Dyer, Fayette, Gibson, Hardeman, Hardin, Haywood, Henderson, Henry, Lake, Lauderdale, Madison, McNairy, Obion, Shelby, Tipton, Weakley—21.

EAST TENNESSEE

ANDERSON COUNTY

ANDERSON COUNTY, named in honor of Judge Joseph Anderson,† was created by Act of the General Assembly, November 6, 1801. It was formed from parts of Knox and Grainger counties. It lies partly in the valley of East Tennessee and partly on the Cumberland plateau. It contains about 450 square miles.

Settlements began in this county about the year 1800 principally by David Hall, Wm. Tunnell, Isaac Coward, Wm. Hogshead, John Chiles, Joseph Hart, Thomas Hart, Joseph Black, Joshua Frost, Collins Roberts, John Garner, Aaron Slover, John Gibbs, Robert Ross, and John Wilson.

The Court of Pleas and Quarter Sessions was organized on December 15, 1801, at the house of John Denham, Sr. The justices of this court were: Hugh Montgomery, Wm. Underwood, Frederick Miller, James Grant, John Kirby, Wm. McKamy, Joseph Sinclair, James Butler, Wm. Standifer, and Solomon Massingale. Wm. Hogshead, who began practice about 1802, was the first lawyer of the county.

The county seat was first named Burrville, in honor of Aaron Burr. By act of the Legislature, in 1809, the name was changed to Clinton in honor of DeWitt Clinton. The site of Clinton was first owned by John Leib, and the lands surrounding it were settled by a colony of Germans, among whom were John Clodfelter, George Bumgartener, and John Leinart. Besides the Germans there were: John McWhirter, John Sutherland, Stephen Bradley, Richard Luallen, James Kirkpatrick, Robert Kirkpatrick, and those mentioned above.

The greater part of the wealth of Anderson County is in its coal and timber lands. Many large mines are in operation.

Statistics of Anderson County: Population, 1920, 18,298. Assessed valuation of taxable property, 1921, $8,701,767. Area, about 360 square miles. Number of farms, 1,677. Railway mileage, 78. County drained by Clinch and Powell Rivers. Its valleys are very fertile. Staple products: wheat, corn, and oats. Live stock industry is very flourishing. County seat, Clinton, about 22 miles northwest of Knoxville; population, 1,409. Has churches, schools, weekly newspaper, two banks,

---
†One of the three judges of the Southwest Territory and successor to William Blount as U. S. Senator, when the latter was expelled from the Senate.

enterprising mercantile establishments, several flourishing mills, and other industries. Coal Creek has a population of 1,204. Scholastic population of county, 6,512; high schools, 7; elementary schools, 55.

BLEDSOE COUNTY

BLEDSOE COUNTY was named in honor of Abraham Bledsoe and was created out of Roane County by act of the Legislature on Nov. 30, 1807. The original county seat was known as Old Madison, six miles from Dunlap and fifteen miles from Pikeville, the present county seat. The first court in the county was held at the residence of a Mr. Thomas. The country surrounding Pikeville is a fine agricultural region. There have been three colleges in or near Pikeville—the People's College, Bledsoe College, and Sequatchie College, the first named of which was chartered in 1871. Sequatchie College was chartered in 1870. Mineral springs, iron ore, and coal are abundant.

Statistics of Bledsoe County: population, 1920, 7,218. Assessed valuation of taxable property, 1921, $4,368,308. Area, 300 square miles. Number of farms, 1,060. Railway mileage, 15. Drained by Sequatchie River and tributaries. Surface somewhat mountainous. Live stock, fruits, and grain crops are principle products. Pasturage excellent. Large areas of fine timber. Corn, oats, and wheat are successfully grown. Coal and limestone abound. Pikeville is the county seat; population, 488. Churches, schools, and weekly newspaper, bank and flourishing business establishments. Scholastic population, 2,946; high schools, 2; elementary schools, 38.

BLOUNT COUNTY

BLOUNT COUNTY is one of the oldest counties in the state, having been erected by the Territorial Legislature on July 11, 1795. It was named for Wm. Blount who was, at that time, the governor of Southwest Territory. It was carved out of Knox County. Its county seat, Maryville, was named for Mary (Grainger) Blount, wife of Gov. William Blount. Its early settlers came principally from Virginia and North Carolina; among them was the mother of Sam Houston, who settled near Maryville in 1806. The settlement of the county really began in 1785, although pioneers had come in some years previously. Among the early settlers were the

Bogles, McCroskeys, McCullochs, Boyds, Cunninghams, Tiptons, McGaugheys, and McMuarrays. They were greatly harassed by the Indians.

The Court of Pleas and Quarter Sessions was organized on the second Monday in September, 1795, at the house of William Weaver. Early lawyers were: John Lowery, Samuel Glass, John Wilkinson, John Garner, and Enoch Parsons. Parsons was defeated for governor, in 1819, by McMinn. Maryville College, one of the best institutions for higher learning in the state, was founded by Rev. Isaac Anderson.

Statistics of Blount County: population, 1920, 28,800. Assessed valuation of taxable property, 1921, $25,370,192. Area, 614 square miles. Number of farms, 2,601. Railway mileage, 98. Drained by the Holston and Little Tennessee Rivers, former navigable for boats. Surface, mountainous with fertile valleys, which abundantly produce wheat, corn, oats, fruit, and live stock. Blount County has more pure-bred Aberdeen-Angus cattle than any other county south of the Ohio River, and many fine herds of pure-bred Poland China hogs. Over 600 silos in the county. Forests of oak and pine. Marble and iron are mined. County seat, Maryville, on railroad; population, 3,739. Has fine schools, two weekly newspapers, three banks, fine churches, and many flourishing industries. Alcoa and Townsend are other prosperous towns. Alcoa has a population of 3,338. Aluminum plant, hosiery mill, foundry, casket factory, 3 woodworking factories, and tannery are among the leading industries of the county. B. R. Cramer is president of the Maryville--Alcoa Chamber of Commerce. Private schools of county are Maryville College, Maryville Polytechnic, and Friendsville Academy. Scholastic population, 10,079; high schools, 2; elementary schools, 86.

BRADLEY COUNTY

BRADLEY COUNTY, named in honor of Col. Edward Bradley of Shelby County, was established by act of the Legislature in 1835. The surface of the county is made up of long valleys running from northeast to southwest with ridges between them. In it is a vast amount of water power, a part of which has been harnessed for commercial use in the Ocoee hydro-electric plant established by the Tennessee Power Company.

The entire section, of which this county is a part, was the

scene of many bloody battles with the Indians in the early pioneer days. In 1819, an agency known as the Cherokee Agency was established on the present site of the city of Charleston, following a treaty with the Cherokee Indians, and Return J. Meigs was appointed the first agent. He held this position until 1823, when he was succeeded by Joseph McMinn, who, in 1821, had completed his third successive term as governor. McMinn died in 1824 and was succeeded by Hugh Montgomery. Simultaneously with the establishment of the Indian agency, Lewis Ross, brother of John Ross, the famous Cherokee Chief, established a store at the agency and remained there until the removal of the Indians in 1838. His wife was a Miss Holt from Virginia. Will T. Hale says: "Previous to 1832 several white men were married to Cherokees, or half breeds, throughout the section. Encroachments were made by the whites in 1832, leading the Indians to believe they would have to abandon their lands. For a consideration some of them proposed to cede their holdings. Chief John Ross and a large following opposed this movement. Major Ridge, his son John, Elias Boudinotte, James Starr, William Rodgers, John Rodgers, and John Watkins, Jr., were in favor of the session, and in 1834, without the sanction of Ross, ceded the lands to the United States. A feud resulted. The first victim was Walker, a well-educated half breed, who, in 1824, had married Miss Emily J. Meigs, a daughter of Return J. Meigs, who lived on a farm just north of the present Cleveland."

"Surveying the Ocoee district was begun in 1837. In November, 1838, Luke Lea was made entry taker, his office being opened at Cleveland. For the first four months the price of land was $7.50 per acre; in the next few months the price was reduced, until in 1841 it sold at one cent per acre. Settlers came in rapidly.

"One of the first preachers was Dr. J. B. McFerrin. Judge Charles J. Keith, in 1836, organized the first court. Among the first lawyers were George W. Rawles, Monroe Campbell, and Levi Trewhitt."

Statistics of Bradley County: population, 1920, 18,652. Assessed valuation of taxable property, 1921, $11,461,376. Area, 280 square miles. Number of farms, 1,836. Railway mileage, 35. Drained by Hiwassee River and tributaries. Surface, hilly and well timbered and soil fertile. Wheat, corn, and live stock are the leading products; and the county is rapidly coming to the front in fruit growing, especially apples, peaches, and strawberries. Soil and climate well adapted to all kinds of fruits. Cleveland, county seat, is on the Southern Railway, 29 miles northeast of Chattanooga; population, 6,522; well supplied with churches and schools; has a large woolen mill and trousers factory, stove foundry, coffin factory, electric light plant, four banks, two weekly newspapers, and a large number of flourishing mercantile establishments. Charleston, Tasso, and McDonald are other towns of Bradley County. Scholastic population of county, 6,936; high schools, 6; elementary schools, 53.

CAMPBELL COUNTY

CAMPBELL COUNTY was erected on September 11, 1806, out of Anderson and Claiborne Counties and was named for Col. Arthur Campbell. Powell's Valley,* famous in the early annals of the state, runs through the entire county on the eastern side. The Court of Pleas and Quarter Sessions was organized at the house of Richard Linville on the first Monday in December, 1806. Settlements had been made, however, ten or more years previously. The site of Jonesboro, the county seat, was owned by Hugh Montgomery, one of the earliest pioneers. His son, Col. L. P. Montgomery,† was killed in the battle of Tohopeka, or Horseshoe Bend in the Creek War.

William Lindsay built the first iron furnace in the county. This was for George Baker. But later he built others which were very successful for that time.

Statistics for Campbell County: population, 1920, 28,265. Assessed valuation of taxable property, 1921, $12,919,026. Area, 488 square miles. Number of farms, 1,892. Railway mileage, 89. Drained by Clinch River and tributaries of Cumberland River. Surface, mountainous and covered with fine forests. Staple products: corn, oats, and grass. Well adapted to live stock industry, which is increasing in importance. Rich coal deposits are found in the county. Jacksboro, county seat, has a population of 638 and is 33 miles from Knoxville. Coal mines are in operation near Jacksboro. Has general stores, churches, schools, a bank, and weekly newspaper. Lafollette, with a population of 3,056, is a flourishing town, with mining industries, banks, weekly newspaper. One of the largest iron furnaces in the South is in operation there. Jellico City, with a population of 1,878, is another flourishing town in the county.

---

*North Carolina gave Richard Henderson 200,000 acres in this valley as a reward for his colonization services.
†Montgomery, Alabama, was named for him.

Scholastic population of county, 11,005; high schools, 9; elementary schools, 80.

CARTER COUNTY

CARTER COUNTY was the first county erected by the first General Assembly of Tennessee in April, 1796, before the state was admitted into the Union, June 1, 1796. It was taken from Washington County, the oldest county in the state and was named for Landon Carter, son of John Carter. The county seat, Elizabethton, was named in honor of his wife, Elizabeth. William Been, the first permanent settler, and other pioneers located on or near the Watauga River in this county. In this valley homes were established by Valentine Sevier, Sr., father of John Sevier, James Robertson, and James P. Taylor, grandfather of Robert L. and Alfred A. Taylor. It is said that James P. Taylor was one of the greatest orators of his time, as well as eminent as a lawyer. His brother-in-law was Thomas D. Love, for whom Robert Love Taylor was given his middle name.

The Court of Pleas and Quarter Sessions was probably organized on July 4, 1776, at the home of Samuel Tipton. The justices of the peace present were: Andrew Greer,* Landon Carter, Nathaniel Taylor, David McNabb, Lochonal Campbell, Guttredge Garland, John Vaught, Joseph Lands, and Reuben Thornton.

Statistics of Carter County: population, 1920, 21,488. Assessed valuation of taxable property, 1921, $7,993,976. Area, 298 square miles. Number of farms, 2,717. Railway mileage, 83. Drained by Watauga River. Surface, mountainous with fertile valleys and well timbered. Corn, oats, grass, and live stock are the staple products. An abundance of iron ore is found in the county. Elizabethton, the county seat, has a population of 2,749. Has three banks, a weekly newspaper, grist, saw, and woolen mills, good churches and schools; iron works in vicinity. Scholastic population of county, 7,712; high schools, 13, elementary schools, 49.

---

*Father of Joseph Greer, the King's Mountain messenger.

CLAIBORNE COUNTY

CLAIBORNE COUNTY was erected on October 29, 1801, and was named for Wm. C. C. Claiborne.† It was formed from Grainger and Hawkins Counties. The Court of Pleas and Quarter Sessions was organized at the house of John Ownes on December 7, 1801, at which time the following-named justices of the peace, appointed by Governor Roane, were qualified: Isaac Lane, Joseph Webster, William Trent, James Chisum, Abraham Lenham, John Wallen, Matthew Sims, John Vanbibber, William Rogers, George Read, C. Newport, John Casey, Joseph Nations, and James Renfro. The courts were held at the houses of magistrates until 1804, when a small courthouse was erected. Cumberland Gap, famous in history, is in this county. Through this gateway in the mountains the pioneers of the early days passed from Virginia, North Carolina, and East Tennessee into Kentucky. The first officers of this court were: Walter Evans, clerk of the court; John Hunt, sheriff; Ezekial Craft, register; Luke or Lew Boyer, or Bowyer, solicitor; Nathaniel Austin, ranger; John Sumpter, constable.

The circuit court was organized in April, 1810, by William Cocke.

The first settlements in the county were made at Big Springs, near Sycamore Creek, in 1794-1795, in Powell's Valley, and along Clinch River.

Tazewell, the county seat, was laid out probably in 1802 or 1803, when the first house in this place was erected. The first merchant was William Graham, who erected the first church.

On October 14, 1802, Bishop Asbury preached "at Hunt's at Claiborne Courthouse."

Statistics of Claiborne County: population, 1920, 23,286. Assessed valuation of taxable property, 1921, $8,549,141. Area, 472 square miles. Number of farms, 3,022. Railway mileage, 37. Drained by the Powell and Clinch Rivers. Surface, generally mountainous and covered with timber. Soil in valleys very fertile. Wheat, corn, oats, and grass are staple products, and the live stock industry is flourishing. Iron, zinc, and lead ores are found in the county, and coal is also mined. Tazewell, the county seat, has a population of 424. Other towns in the county are New Tazewell, Lone Mountain, Hoop, and Hartranft. Tazewell has a bank, schools, churches, and a weekly newspaper. Scholastic population, 8,994; high schools, 2; elementary schools, 100.

---

†One of the first judges of the superior court and one of the first representatives in Congress from Tennessee.

COCKE COUNTY

COCKE COUNTY was erected on October 9, 1797, and named in honor of William Cocke.‡ It was carved out of Jefferson County. The first settlements were made along the Nollichucky River in 1783. Among the early settlers were: George McNutt, John McNabb, John Gilliland, William Lillard, Samuel Odell, and Daniel Adams. For the first ten years the Indians gave them much trouble. The first church was organized by the Baptists in 1794, about a year after the Indian depredations ceased. Eminent lawyers of the early days were: Thomas Gray, William Garrett, and Tilghman A. Howard, the last-named of whom moved to Indiana and became a well-known general in the Civil War.

Statistics of Cocke County: population, 1920, 20,782. Assessed valuation of taxable property, 1921, $11,402,158. Area, 458 square miles. Number of farms, 2,800. Railway mileage, 48. Drained by the French Broad and Nollichucky Rivers. Smoky Mountain extends along the southeastern border of the county, and this section is covered with timber. Soil in valleys is very fertile. The staple products are: corn, wheat, grass, and live stock. Newport, the county seat, is on the Southern Railway, 50 miles east of Knoxville; has a population of 2,753, several churches and schools, two weekly newspapers, two banks, cotton and flour mills, and a canning establishment, the largest of its kind in the South. Scholastic population of the county, 6,652; high schools, 1; elementary schools, 86.

CUMBERLAND COUNTY

CUMBERLAND COUNTY was erected in 1856 from parts of White, Van Buren, Bledsoe, Rhea, Roane, Morgan, and Putnam. It was named for the Cumberland Mountains, on whose crest it lies; and they, as well as the Cumberland River, were named by Dr. Thomas Walker in honor of the Duke of Cumberland. The first county court was held at Crossville, the county seat, located near the center of the county.

The fruits and vegetables of this county, as well as the mountain counties, generally, possess peculiar excellences of freedom from insect pests as well as beauty and flavor. As early as the founding of the county itself this fact was known;

---

‡He and William Blount were the first U. S. Senators from Tennessee.

and J. W. Dodge, who lived near Crossville, took many prizes for his apples.

Statistics of Cumberland County: population, 1920, 10,094. Assessed valuation of taxable property, 1921, $5,232,844. Area, nearly 800 square miles. Number of farms, 1,267. Railway mileage, 58. Situated centrally upon the Cumberland Plateau at an average elevation of nearly 2,000 feet. It is drained by the affluents of both the Cumberland and the Tennessee Rivers. The surface is gently undulating, generally covered with timber. Luxuriant native grasses make it one of the best counties in the state for grazing cattle. There are many deposits of coal in the county and several mines are in operation. Land is excellently adapted to truck and fruit growing. Soil especially suited to Irish potatoes. Crossville, the county seat, with a population of 948, is on the Tennessee Central Railway. It has good churches, schools, a bank, a weekly newspaper, and is the center of rapidly developing coal and timber industries. Scholastic population of county, 3,855; high schools, 1; elementary school, 59.

GRAINGER COUNTY

GRAINGER COUNTY was the second county created by the first Legislature on April 22, 1796. It was named in honor of Mrs. William Blount, whose maiden name was Mary Grainger. It was formed from Hawkins and Knox Counties. The county seat is Rutledge, named for George Rutledge, a prominent pioneer. Some of the pioneers were: Col. James Ore,* the Senters, Crabtrees, Hendersons, Taylors, Johnsons, Bassetts, Lebons, Lowes, Jarnagans, and Tates. Settlement began about 1784.

The county seat was not located until 1801 when the courthouse was erected. But the county court was organized on June 13, 1796 (less than two months after the county was created) at the house of Benjamin McCarty, with the following-named magistrates appointed by Governor Sevier: Thomas Henderson, Elijah Chisum, James Blair, John Estes, Phelps Read, Benjamin McCarty, James Moore, John Bowen, John Kidwell, John Sims, William Thompson, and Major Lea.

Statistics of Grainger County: population, 1921, 13,369. Assessed valuation of taxable property, 1921, $5,980.954. Area, 300 square miles. Number of farms, 2,257. Railway mileage, 47. Drained by Clinch and Holston Rivers. Has a high ridge

---

*He commanded the expedition from the Cumberland settlements against the Indians at Nickajack Cave and Running Water in 1794.

surface called Clinch Mountain. County is well timbered; soil in valleys very fertile. Corn, oats, wheat, grass, and live stock are the staple products. Fine iron ore deposits are found in the county. County has ample railway mileage. Tate Spring and other noted mineral springs are in this county. Rutledge, the county seat, is near the base of Clinch Mountain, about 33 miles northeast of Knoxville, and has a population of about 600, two banks, schools, churches, weekly newspaper, and flourishing business establishments. Other towns are Washburn, Noeton, and Idol. Scholastic population of county, 4,480; high schools, 5; elementary schools, 56.

GREENE COUNTY

GREENE COUNTY was created by the State of North Carolina from a part of Washington County in April 1783, and was named in honor of Gen. Nathaniel Greene.† Settlements were begun in 1778, or earlier. Some of the early settlers were: Anthony Moore, who located near Henderson's Station, Daniel Kennedy, and Henry Earnest who were greatly interested in the establishment of the Methodist Church named Ebenezer, said to be the first organization of this sect in the State of Tennessee. It was located on the Nollichucky River.

On the third Monday in August, 1783, the Court of Pleas and Quarter Sessions was organized at the house of Robert Carr, near the Big Spring, in Greeneville. The magistrates present were: Joseph Hardin, John Newman, George Dougherty, James Houston, Amos Bird, and Asahel Rawlings.

From the very beginning much attention was paid to education. Greeneville College, founded by Hezekiah Balch, was chartered in 1794, and Tusculum College was established in 1818 by Dr. Samuel Doak. Some Quakers settled in this county, many of whom became greatly interested in emancipation of slaves.

Statistics of Greene County: population, 1920, 32,824. Assessed valuation of taxable property, 1921, $20,501,539. Area, 580 square miles. Number of farms, 5, 313. Railway mileage, 31. Drained by Nollichucky River and Lick Creek. Surface partly mountainous and well timbered. Valleys are very fertile. Staple products are: corn, wheat, oats, grass, tobacco, and live stock. The tobacco industry has developed rapidly in the last few years, a fine quality of burley being produced. The Southern Railway intersects the county. Fine deposits of limestone

---

†North Carolina also gave him 25,000 acres of land, located in Maury County.

and iron are found in the county. Greeneville, the county seat, has a population of 3,775 and is on the Southern Railway. Greeneville is a large tobacco market with six large warehouses, four banks, hosiery mill, chair factory, two wagon factories, tobacco factory, stemmery and redrying plant, one of the largest proprietary medicine concerns in the South, three flour mills and other industries, a weekly and a daily newspaper. Other towns are: Baileyton, Mosheim, Chuckey, and Midway. There are several commercial organizations, including the Burley Association, C. H. Bewlry, secretary; Rotary Club, J. H. Rader, secretary. Greene County has 300 miles of pike roads and 200 miles of graded roads. The county is very progressive in educational matters, having five Presbyterian mission schools, Tusculum College, and private schools in Greeneville. The public school system is said to be one of the finest in the state. Scholastic population of county, 12,895; high schools 8; elementary schools, 100.

HAMBLEN COUNTY

HAMBLEN COUNTY was created on May 31, 1870, and was named for Hezekiah Hamblen. It was formed from parts of Grainger, Jefferson, and Hawkins Counties. The first settlement in what is now Hamblen County was made by Robert McFarland and Alexander Outlaw in 1783. They located at the "bend" of the Nollichucky.

One of the historic spots in this county is "Hayslope," the handsome old home of one of the pioneer settlers, Col. James Roddye, one of the signers of the first Constitution of Tennessee. The town of Russellville is built on a tract of land awarded Colonel Roddye for service in the Battle of Kings Mountain, and was named for his second wife, Miss Russell.

Morristown was named for the Morris family of whom three brothers, Gideon, Daniel, and Absalom, settled near it, having gone thither from their former home on the Watauga.

Through the territory now included in Hamblen extended the stage road from Knoxville to Abingdon, Va., which road was constructed as early as 1793; and along this road most of the settlers located, among them William Chaney, Thomas Daggett, Phelps Redd, Richard Thompson, Isaac Martin, and John Crockett, father of David Crockett.

On October 3, 1770, the county court was organized in an old storehouse in Morristown. The magistrates present were: S. P. Nixon, L. D. Milligan, L. F. Leiper, C. L. Gregory,

George McFarland, R. M. Hamblen, A. J. Donelson, Alexander Williams, Jonathan Noe, G. W. Carmichael, C. J. Burnett, D. S. Noe, R. P. Sharp, William Felkner, S. M. Heath, James Hale, W. B. Ninnie, S. J. Couch, I. P. Haun, and Samuel Smith.

Statistics of Hamblen County: population, 1920, 15,056. Assessed valuation of taxable property, 1921, $11,184,675. Area, 150 square miles. Number of farms, 1,564. Railway mileage, 31. Drained by the Holston and French Broad Rivers. The surface is undulating and the soil fertile. The Southern Railway intersects the county. Principal products are grass, fruit, live stock, and poultry. It is one of the best fruit counties in the eastern section of the state, and the poultry industry is also of large proportions, Morristown, the county seat, being one of the largest poultry markets in the South. Morristown, on the Southern Railway and the Holston River, has a population of 5,875, has splendid churches and schools, daily and weekly newspapers, three banks, manufacturing establishments, and prosperous mercantile concerns. Scholastic population of the county, 5,416; high schools, 5; elementary schools, 35.

HAMILTON COUNTY

HAMILTON COUNTY was erected out of Rhea County by the act of the Legislature passed on October 25, 1819, "that the territory southwest of Rhea and south and east of Bledsoe and Marion Counties should constitute a county by the name of Hamilton, in honor and to perpetuate the memory of the late Alexander Hamilton, Secretary of the Treasury of the United States." The act recites the boundaries of the new county which, of course, were somewhat changed when James County was carved out of portions of Hamilton and Bradley Counties on January 27, 1871. On April 14, 1919, however, an act* was passed abolishing James County and transferring to Hamilton the territory formerly embraced in James County.

About half of Hamilton County, when first formed, and all of the county on the left bank of the Tennessee River lay within the territory of the Cherokee nation. The Indian title was extinguished by a treaty concluded between the United States and the Cherokees on December 29, 1835.

The county seat was first established at Dallas, but, by an election in 1840, the seat was transferred to Harrison, named after Gen. William H. Harrison, subsequently elected Presi-

*Private Acts of 1919, Chapter 695, p. 2129.

dent. By an election in November, 1870, the county seat was transferred from Harrison to Chattanooga.

Prof. J. B. Brown, State Superintendent of Public Instruction, 1921-1923, in an article published in the Nashville American on June 26, 1910, said of Hamilton County, besides other things:

"The topography of the county is exceedingly varied. The larger portion toward the northwest is mountainous and wild, while the remainder, about two-fifths, is for the most part lowland, lying in the valley of the Tennessee River or of some of its tributaries from the northwest. Walden's Ridge and Raccoon Mountain occupy a small portion of the western border. Missionary Ridge, rising to a height of 500 feet above the valley, Walden's Ridge, 1,500 feet, and Lookout Mountain to a maximum height of 1,700 feet above the low water in the Tennessee are the chief elevations of the county. The climate of Hamilton County averages 42 degrees in winter, 72 degrees in summer, and 60 degrees in spring and autumn.

"The geology of the county is very simple, but very interesting from an economical point of view. Many formations are present in the county, some of the strata belonging to the very early formations. Limestone predominates, existing in many forms. The coal and iron deposits are most important. Coal is found in great abundance in Raccoon Mountain, Walden's Ridge, and Lookout Mountain.

"The natural products of the forests are greatly varied. The oak, the most abundant growth, is found throughout the county; other kinds of timber that grow plentifully are the ash, black walnut, beech, birch, cherry, cedar, hickory, maple, and white and yellow poplar. The short-leaf yellow pine is also found in some portions of the county. Clover and different varieties of herds-grass grow luxuriantly. The leading crops are corn, wheat, potatoes, broom corn, sorghum—all of which grow to perfection in this climate.

"Garden vegetables and horticultural products of all kinds, except some varieties of the grape, find here a congenial soil and atmosphere.

"It is believed to be true that the first settlers of this county were Scotchmen, who came here immediately after the close of the Revolutionary War. Many of them married Indian wives and were incorporated into the Cherokee Nation. The name of Daniel Rose is one of the very first associated with the history of Hamilton County. Others are: Robert Patterson, Patrick Martin, William Lauderdale, and Charles Gamble, who became the first sheriff.

"Others who belonged to a later period are: Hasten Poe, Asahel Rawlings, James Cozby, John Russell, Joseph Rogers, David Beck, John Brown, John Taylor, Nimrod Moore, Jackson Jenkins, Jonathan Springer, D. R. Rawlings, William Walker, and Crispian Eli Shelton."

Chattanooga

The country around Chattanooga was occupied by the Cherokee Indians until the year 1837, when a post office was first established at that point which was then called Ross' Landing, after either Chief John Ross* or his brother who established a store there. In that same year a town was laid off and divided into lots and the name Chattanooga was given to it. It was incorporated as a town in 1841 and as a city in 1851.

The meaning of the name Chattanooga has been a mooted question for many years. Most historians and others say it means "Eagle's nest." In the Chattanooga Daily Times of July 1, 1903, appeared an article written by Miss Zella Armstrong on the origin and meaning of the word Chattanooga. In it she said:

"In a correspondence with the Hon. Joshua Ross concerning his distinguished uncle, Chief John, who left his impress deep upon this historic country, I inquired what could be learned among the living Cherokees upon this subject. Promptly came the answer, and it forever clears the romance and the mystery from our 'eagle's nest.' Says Mr. Ross: 'My own impression is that Chattanooga is derived from a Creek Indian word, as "Creek Path" is not many miles distant. I find in the living Creek language "Chat-to-to-noo-gee," the literal meaning of which is "rock coming to a point; a cliff or bluff or overhanging rock," as is found at the point of Lookout Mountain.'"

The University of Chattanooga, in which all the people of this city take so just a pride, was started as the East Tennessee Wesleyan College at Athens in 1867. Later it was called Grant University and still later the University of Chattanooga which has a College of Arts and Science and a School of Law.

The many points of interest and scenic grandeur in and around Chattanooga attract thousands of visitors and tourists from all parts of the country. The most noted of these are: Chickamauga National Park, Missionary Ridge, Orchard

---

*The house occupied by John Ross still stands in Rossville, a suburb of Chattanooga.

Knob, National Cemetery, Confederate Cemetery, Lookout Mountain with its $100,000 cable incline 4,750 feet long, Signal Mountain, and Walden's Ridge.

Statistics of Hamilton County: population, 1920, 115,954. Assessed valuation taxable property, 1921, $140,321,440. (Hamilton County now includes the territory formerly embraced in James County, the latter having been abolished by act of the General Assembly.) Area, 785 square miles. Number of farms, 2,480. Railway mileage, 146. Drained by Tennessee River and tributaries. County has a varied and fertile soil, well adapted to the growth of all kinds of crops, including the different grains, grasses, fruits, and vegetables. Truck farming is carried on extensively in the vicinity of Chattanooga, and there is a large business in the shipment of early vegetables to the northern markets. The length of the growing season makes it possible for the truck farmer to grow as many as three crops in one year on the same ground, and a ready and convenient market is found at good prices. Large shipments of strawberries are made every year. There is a profitable business in poultry and dairying. The staple products are corn, wheat, oats, fruits, cattle, and hogs. The county is traversed by the Nashville, Chattanooga & St. Louis Railway, the Southern Railway, the Cincinnati Southern, and there are other roads entering from the South. The county has a fine system of public highways. Lookout Mountain is situated in the southern part of the county and is famed for its magnificent scenery and historic interest. Chickamauga National Park is near, as is Missionary Ridge. All these were battle grounds during the Civil War. Chattanooga, the county seat, with a population of 57,895, is one of the most progressive cities in the South and is located on the Tennessee River at the base of Lookout Mountain. Its river and railroad connections furnish first-class transportation facilities. Ten railroads enter the city. Chattanooga has many large manufacturing industries, two daily newspapers, several banks of large resources, and all the business interests of a large city. Scholastic population of county, 35,887; high schools, 14; elementary schools, 94. Information will be furnished by the Chamber of Commerce, Chattanooga, Tenn.

HANCOCK COUNTY

HANCOCK COUNTY was erected on January 7, 1844, and was named for John Hancock. It was formed from parts of Hawkins and Claiborne Counties. Because of some constitutional objections* it was not organized until 1846, when a commission was appointed to have the county resurveyed so that the rights of other counties might not be interfered with. The personnel of that commission was: A. P. McCarty, Anderson Campbell, Richard Mitchell, William Nichol, of Hawkins County, and James Ritchie, James Fulkerson, John Farmer, Marshall Brewer, and Alexander Bates, of Claiborne County. These commissioners were also authorized to organize the county. Sneedville was selected as the county seat and was named for John L. T. Sneed, the eminent lawyer who successfully defended the suit brought against the new county for running its line within twelve miles of Rogersville, the county seat of Hawkins County. The first court was held at the house of Alexander Campbell.

Settlements began as early as 1795. Some of the early pioneers were: William McGee, John Ray, Enos Matthias, William McCully, Daniel Slavins, John Givins, Alexander Treat, Solomon Mitchell, John Amis, and Lincoln Amis. Of the early settlers, M. E. Testerman says: "The county was settled largely by immigrants from Virginia and North Carolina, and many of these were of the very best blood of the world; and no county in the state, population and area considered, has in the same length of time produced more men of worth and note than Hancock."

Hancock was one of the first counties in the state to establish a system of public schools, for which its people have always responded generously. This is one of the few counties in the state in which Melungeons dwell.

Statistics of Hancock County: population, 1920, 10,454. Assessed valuation of taxable property, 1921, $2,733,197. Area, 260 square miles. Number of farms, 1,820. Railway mileage, none. Drained by the Clinch River. Its surface partly mountainous and covered with a fine growth of timber. It is rich in all kinds of minerals, including iron ore, lead, zinc, marble, granite, ochre, phosphates, coal, and silver. Corn, wheat, oats, and live stock are staple products. Sneedville, the county seat, has a population of about 500 and is located on the Clinch River, 50 miles northeast of Knoxville. It has good churches,

---

*The Constitution of the State prohibited the establishment of a new county whose line encroached within twelve miles of the county seat of the county from which any of the territory of the new county was taken.

schools, bank, newspaper, and flourishing business houses. Scholastic population, 3,833; high schools, 1; elementary schools, 49.

HAWKINS COUNTY

HAWKINS COUNTY was formed from Sullivan County by the State of North Carolina in 1786, while the State of Franklin was concurrently functioning. It was named for Benjamin Hawkins, who, as United States Senator, conjointly with Senator Samuel Johnston, executed, on February 25, 1790, the deed which transferred what is now Tennessee to the United States. Its early settlers came principally from North Carolina and Virginia, with some from Pennsylvania and a sprinkling from New England. The first settlements were made in Carter's Valley about the time of the first settlements on the Watauga. Prominent among them were the Kinkeads, Loves, Longs, Mulkeys, Carter, and Parker, who established a store, Thomas Gillenwaters, Robert Lucas, Thomas Amis, who came about 1781 and built a stone house, a store, a blacksmith shop, a distillery, a saw mill and grist mill and kept a tavern, William Cocke, who settled at Mulberry Grove about 1780, Joseph McMinn, Governor of Tennessee, 1815-1821, Peter Parsons, Orville Bradley, John A. McKinney, Pleasant M. Miller, and Samuel Powell.

From the first they took a great interest in education. Notable teachers in the early days were: John Long, 1783; William Evans, 1784; James King, 1786; Samuel B. Hawkins, 1796.

Rogersville, the county seat, was established by the State of North Carolina and was one of the last acts of the Legislature of that state prior to the act of cession in 1789. It was named for Joseph Rogers, the first settler at that place. The old Rogers tavern was one of the most famous taverns of the early days. Andrew Jackson and other notables made it their stopping place.

The Knoxville Gazette, the first newspaper published in Tennessee, was first issued in Rogersville by George Roulstone in 1791. The Railroad Gazette, the first newspaper devoted exclusively to internal improvement published in the United States, was established at Rogersville in 1843.

Statistics of Hawkins County: population, 1920, 22,918. Assessed valuation of taxable property, 1921, $12,741,069. Area, 490 square miles. Number of farms, 3,314. Railway mileage, 51. Drained by the Clinch River. Its surface is hilly and valleys very fertile. The county is covered with a growth of fine timber, including hardwoods common to the South. Minerals found are: iron, zinc, lead, barytes, magnesia, iron pyrites, salt, marble. Corn, wheat, oats, grass, and live stock are staple products. Fruit growing is developing into a profitable industry in the county. Poultry and dairy products are important industries. The Southern Railway passes through the southern portion of the county. The county has good roads and many fine mineral springs. Rogersville, the county seat, on the Southern Railway, has a population of 1,402. Has good churches and schools, banks and newspapers, and many prosperous business establishments. Scholastic population of county, 9,620; high schools, 5; elementary schools, 95.

JEFFERSON COUNTY

JEFFERSON COUNTY was erected on June 11, 1792, by William Blount when governor of the Territory south of the River Ohio. It was formed from portions of Greene and Hawkins Counties and was named in honor of Thomas Jefferson. The first settlers came in 1783. Among them were: Robert McFarland, Alexander Outlaw, Thomas Jarnagin, James Hill, Wesley White, James Randolph, Joseph Copeland, Robert Gentry, James Hubbard, Matthew Wallace, James Roddye, Richard Rankin, Thomas Snoddy, Parmenas Taylor, Hugh Kelso, Adam Meek, and George Doherty, most of whom were prominently identified with the early history of Tennessee.

Dandridge, established in 1793, was selected for the county seat, and the first Court of Pleas and Quarter Sessions was organized at the house of Jeremiah Matthews with the following magistrates in attendance: Alexander Outlaw, James Roddey, John Blackborn, James Lea, Joseph Wilson, Josiah Wilson, Andrew Henderson, Amos Balch, and William Cox.

The oldest church is the Hopewell Presbyterian Church, established in 1785.

Among the interesting records of Jefferson County is the record that, on October 22, 1805, David Crockett was licensed to marry Margaret Elder. However, after all the arrangements had been made Miss Elder refused to marry him. But it seems that the wound was not irremediable, for on August 12, 1806, a license was issued to him to marry Polly Findley.

Statistics of Jefferson County: population, 1920, 17,677. Assessed valuation of taxable property, 1921, $11,052.203. Area, 310 square miles. Number of farms, 2,209. Railway mileage, 22. Drained by the Holston and French Broad Rivers. Surface marked by high ridges and fertile valleys. It has a fine timber growth, including the hardwoods. Iron ore and limestone are found in paying quantities. Wheat, corn, oats, grasses, fruits, and live stock are staple products. The Southern Railway intersects the county seat, lies three miles north of the French Broad River. It has a population of 439 and is a flourishing town with good schools, churches, banks, newspaper, and commercial and manufacturing enterprises. Other towns are: Mossy Creek and Jefferson City. Scholastic population of county, 6,555; high schools, 4; elementary schools, 66.

JOHNSON COUNTY

JOHNSON COUNTY was erected in 1836 out of a part of Carter County and was named in honor of Cave Johnson. It is the extreme eastern county of the state and is famous for its beautiful mountain scenery. F. C. Dougherty, in his article published in the Nashville American of June 26, 1910, says:

"Have you been up in Johnson, 'The Land of the Sky,'
Where a banquet of glory is spread for the eye,
And the breezes that float o'er mountain's tall peak,
Give back the invalid the rose to this cheek?"

The first settlement was made in 1770, or possibly a little earlier, as some investigators think that one Honeycut, whom James Robertson found on Roane Creek, near its confluence with the Watauga River, on his exploration trip from North Carolina, had preceded William Been.

At an early period Nathaniel Taylor also came to Roane Creek where he established iron works. He was an ancestor of Alfred A. Taylor and Robert L. Taylor; and Taylorville, the first county seat, was named for him. Some years after the War between the States, Roderick R. Random, then State Senator, succeeded in having the county seat changed to Mountain City.

The first session of the county court was held on May 2, 1836, with the following magistrates: John Ward, Thomas Johnson, A. L. Wilson, Jared Arendill, J. W. Warren, Joseph Robinson, James W. Wright, A. Wilson, James Brown, Jesse Cole, Levi Heath, M. M. Wagner, John Dugger, Sr., and Philip Shull.

Statistics of Johnson County: population, 1920, 12,230. Assessed valuation of taxable property, 1921, $4,037,685. Area,

340 square miles. Number of farms, 1,672. Railway mileage, 18. Watauga River drains a part of the county. Surface is mountainous with fertile valleys. Grazing fine for sheep and cattle. Large part of the county is covered with a fine growth of timber. Corn, wheat, oats, and grasses are staple products. Iron ore is found in the county. Mountain City, the county seat, has a population of 724 and is a flourishing town with good schools and churches, banks, weekly newspaper, and prosperous commercial establishments. Scholastic population of county, 4,067; high schools, 1; elementary schools, 42.

KNOX COUNTY

KNOX COUNTY was erected on June 11, 1792, out of Greene and Hawkins Counties and was named in honor of Gen. Henry Knox, Secretary of War in Washington's cabinet. On the 16th of the same month, says Ramsey,* "James White, John Sawyers, Hugh Beard, John Adair, George McNutt, Jeremiah Jack, John Kerns, James Cozby, John Evans, Samuel Newell, William Wallace, Thomas McCulloch, William Hamilton, David Craig, and William Lowry presented a commission from Governor Blount appointing them Justices of the Peace for Knox County, and appeared before the Honorable David Campbell, Esq., who, in the presence of Governor Blount, administered to each of them an oath to support the Constitution of the United States, and also an oath of office.

"Charles McClung also produced a Commission from the Governor, appointing him Clerk of Knox County, and he was in like manner qualified.

"Thomas Chapman, also, as Register.

"June 25, Robert Houston, in like manner, commissioned and qualified as sheriff." . . .

"The first court held was on the 16th of July, 1792. Present—James White, Samuel Newell, David Craig, and Jeremiah Jack. James White was appointed chairman."

The following men eminent in the history of Tennessee were qualified and admitted to the practice of law in this court: Luke Bowyer, Alexander Outlaw, Joseph Hamilton, Archibald Roane, Hopkins Lacy, John Rhea, and James Reese.

Knoxville, the county seat of Knox County, was founded, named, and laid out in 1791. The date of the contract between James White, the founder of Knoxville, and the commissions

*Annals of Tennessee, page 568.

on behalf of the purchasers of lots was October 3, 1791. But it was not until February, 1792, that much improvement was undertaken, and June 11, 1792, is the date of the founding of Knoxville. Before the contract was made with the purchasers of the lots and the naming of the town as Knoxville, this place was called White's Fort, which was a frontier stronghold.

There were two eminent men, named James White, in early Tennessee history; and, as they were contemporaneous for a time, they are frequently mistaken for each even by historians.

One of these notable characters was Dr. James White, of Davidson County, who was chosen as the Territorial representative in Congress, and the other was Gen. James White, founder of Knoxville and father of Hugh Lawson White.

General White donated the land upon which was located Blount College,† the First Presbyterian Church, and the adjoining cemetery.

When William Blount received his commission as Governor of the Southwest Territory on August 7, 1790, he immediately left for the scene of his future activities and in the autumn of that year made his residence at the home of William Cobb in the fork of the Holston and Watauga Rivers. Here were his court and his capital until in 1792 when he made Knoxville the capital of the territory.

When Tennessee became the sixteenth state of the Union in 1796, Knoxville was made the capital. Section 1, of Article X, of the first Constitution of the State, adopted in 1796, reads: "Knoxville shall be the seat of government until the year one thousand eight hundred and two." It continued as the capital, however, until 1807, when the Seventh General Assembly met at Kingston, but adjourned to Knoxville after two days. Knoxville remained the capital until 1813 when the Legislature met at Nashville for the first time. The only time subsequently when Knoxville was the capital was when the Legislature met there in 1817.

Statistics of Knox County: population, 1920, 112,926. Assessed valuation of taxable property, 1921, $119,642,106. Area, 612 square miles. Number of farms, 3,969. Railway mileage, 120. Drained by the Tennessee River and its tributaries. The farms are very rich and productive along these streams and in the other valleys. Improved valley lands range between $50 and $150 per acre. Fine macadamized roads reach every section of the county. Lands around Knoxville are well adapted

---

†Named in honor of Governor Wm. Blount, chartered in 1794, later named East Tennessee University, and now the University of Tennessee.

to truck farming. All kinds of early vegetables are grown and find a ready market and are shipped north. Knoxville, the county seat, with a population of 77,718, is one of the most enterprising and flourishing cities in the state, is the seat of the State University, and there are many other fine schools. It has many manufacturing and industrial establishments, splendid banking institutions, and a large jobbing trade with the eastern section of the state and with Kentucky and other states. Many fine marble quarries are operated in the vicinity of Knoxville, the quality of the marble being such that it is in demand all over the country. Railroads entering the city are: the Southern, the Louisville and Nashville, and the Knoxville, Seviersville & Eastern. Knoxville has two daily newspapers and several class publications. The scholastic population of the county is 42,995; high schools, 15; elementary schools, 101.

LOUDON COUNTY

LOUDON COUNTY was erected on May 27, 1870, from parts of Roane, Monroe, and Blount counties and was named in commemoration of Fort Loudon, which, in turn, was named for the Earl of Loudon, commander-in-chief, in 1756, of the British forces in America and Governor of Virginia. It lies on both sides of the Tennessee about twenty-nine miles southwest of Knoxville. This county was established in accordance with especial provisions embodied in Section 4, Article X of the Constitution of 1870.

Early settlers were: Henry Bogard, Jacob Gardengill, John Browder, Benjamin Prater, William B. Lenoir, James Blair, Samuel Blair, William Blair, Jesse Eldridge, Simeon Eldridge.

The Presbyterians erected the first church in this county in 1823. Its pastor was Dr. Isaac Anderson, a teacher of Sam Houston.

Statistics of Loudon County: population, 1920, 16,275. Assessed valuation of taxable property, 1921, $10,018,424. Area, 256 square miles. Number of farms, 1,396; railway mileage, 29. Drained by the Little Tennessee River. Surface is hilly, but soil fertile. There is a fine timber growth in the county. Good opportunities in the county for marble and furniture industries. The county is intersected by the Southern Railway. Loudon, the county seat, has a population of about 1,000, is a flourishing town on the Southern Railway and the Tennessee River, and has splendid schools, churches, weekly newspaper, manufacturing establishments, and stores, bank, etc. Lenoir

City, with a population of 4,210, has several manufacturing establishments, including car works, and is a prosperous town. Scholastic population of the county, 5,488; high schools, 4; elementary schools, 38.

McMINN COUNTY

McMINN COUNTY was created on November 5, 1819, out of lands ceded by the Cherokee Indians to the United States in that year, and was named for Joseph McMinn, who was Governor at that time.

McMinn, Monroe, and Bradley Counties embraced the largest and best portions of the land thus ceded. "A new judicial circuit was established in lower East Tennessee, composed of seven counties, of which McMinn was one; and the Hon. Charles F. Keith, then a leading lawyer of Jefferson County, Tennessee, was elected the first judge and held the first Circuit Court in the county at the house of John Walker, in the town of Calhoun, on the Hiwasse River, fourteen miles southwest from Athens, the present county seat, on the first Monday of March, 1820."*

Maj. John Walker was part Cherokee and laid off the town of Calhoun on land allotted him and named it for John C. Calhoun. In 1821-1822, the town of Athens was laid off, and in 1823 the courts of the county were moved there. Noted members of the Athens bar were: Return J. Meigs, Spencer Jarnagin, Thomas Campbell, later Clerk of the House of Representatives in Congress, and J. W. M. Brazeale, the historian.

Early settlers in McMinn County were: A. R. Turk, E. P. Owen, John Cowan, George Colville, and Eli Sharp.

After he had served his third successive term as Governor, McMinn was appointed agent to the Cherokee Indians and at his death was buried in the yard of the Presbyterian Church at Calhoun which was built in 1823.

A pretty romance is told of the marriage of Miss Emily Meigs, daughter of Return J. Meigs, to the son of John Walker. The young man was very handsome, but as he had Cherokee blood her father opposed the union. So they eloped. But as he was a Cherokee chief he was compelled to placate his people by espousing an Indian girl, named Nancy Bushyhead. He was murdered by two Indians as he was returning from the council which decided upon the Cherokee cession.

John H. Reagan, postmaster-general of the Confederacy,

---
*Killebrew's Resources of Tennessee, page 580.

who also achieved renown in Texas, and Senator John T. Morgan, of Alabama, were natives of McMinn County.

Statistics of McMinn County: population, 1920, 25,133. Assessed valuation of taxable property, 1921, $11,063,543. Area, 452 square miles. Number of farms, 2,654. Railway mileage, 56. Drained by the Hiwassee River and tributaries. Fine growth of timber and soil very fertile in the valleys. The Louisville and Nashville and Southern Railways intersect the county. Corn, wheat, oats, and grasses are staple products. The county has a fine system of public highways. Athens, the county seat, has a population of 2,580 and is on the Southern Railway 55 miles northeast of Chattanooga and 55 miles from Knoxville. It has a fine electric light plant, splendid churches and schools, including a branch of the University of Chattanooga; two newspapers, flour mill, two box factories, roller mill, hosiery mills, table and chair factory, two planing mills, concrete tile plant, etc. Etowah, with a population of 2,516, is on the main line of the Louisville and Nashville Railroad, 60 miles south of Knoxville. It is headquarters of the Atlanta Division of the Louisville and Nashville Railroad. This town is fourteen years old and has had the most remarkable growth of any town in the state. Etowah has two banks, one newspaper, fine electric light plant and water plant, manufacturing and commercial establishments, and is a rich agricultural section. Scholastic population of the county, 8,858; high schools, 6; elementary schools, 97. Other towns in McMinn: Riceville, Calhoun, Niota, Englewood, each of which has a bank.

MARION COUNTY

MARION COUNTY was erected in 1817 out of the Cherokee lands and was named for Gen. Francis Marion. It was organized in 1818 at the town of Liberty which remained the county seat until 1820 when it was removed to Jasper.

Marion County is noted for its mineral springs and for its coal and iron deposits.

Statistics of Marion County: population, 1920, 17,402. Assessed valuation of taxable property, 1921, $12,448,090. Area, 500 square miles. Number of farms, 1,037. Railway mileage, 68. Drained by the Tennessee and Sequatchie Rivers. Surface broken by high ridges running parallel with the Cumberland Mountains. Soil is fertile and there is a fine timber growth. Staple products are corn, wheat, cotton, oats, hay, and live stock. Coal is mined in considerable quantity. Jasper, the county seat, with a population of 728, is situated on the Sequatchie River and the Nashville, Chattanooga & St. Louis Railway and has good churches, schools, weekly newspaper and prosperous business establishments. South Pittsburg, with a population of 2,356, and Whitwell are other flourishing towns. Scholastic population of county, 6,981; high schools, 3; elementary schools, 58.

MEIGS COUNTY

MEIGS COUNTY also was carved out of the territory ceded to the United States by the Cherokees in 1819. It was erected by act of the Legislature in 1836 and named for Return J. Meigs. This treaty is frequently spoken of as the Hiwassee Purchase. Meigs County was formed from parts of Rhea, Roane, Hamilton, and McMinn Counties.

Some romantic interest attaches to this county in connection with Sam Houston as it is supposed to have been the home of Chief Jolly of the Cherokees who adopted Sam Houston and with whom Houston spent much time when a boy. It is a tradition that the Chief's home was on Jolly's Island at the mouth of Hiwassee River.

Under the treaty of 1819 the country north of Hiwassee River was opened to settlement and was attached to Rhea County until 1836. As the Tennessee River then divided Rhea County, an unsuccessful effort to create a new county had been made some years previously. Hon. Miles Vernon was a resident of what is now Meigs County and, being a member of the State Senate, became an active and finally successful advocate of the creation of the county desired. The act, as originally passed by the Senate, named the new county Vernon, in honor of Senator Vernon, and the county seat Reagan, after James Reagan, Senator from McMinn County. The House of Representatives, however, changed these names and during the discussion the name DeKalb was suggested for the county; but finally agreement was arrived at on Meigs for the county, and Decatur. in honor of Commodore Stephen Decatur, for the county seat.

The act which created the county was approved January 21, 1836, and the first county court was organized on May 2, 1836, at the house of John Stewart, three miles north of the present county seat, which was later located by commissioners appointed by the Legislature on May 16, 1836. This action took place at the residence of James Lillard and the site itself was on land donated by him and by Leonard Brooks. Money for erecting the first county buildings was raised by the sale of lots, and the expense in connection with the sale was $49.50, of which $1.50 was for "liquor furnished by West at divers times."

Statistics of Meigs County: population, 1920, 6,077. Assessed valuation of taxable property, 1921, $2,056,327. Area, 200 square miles. Number of farms, 935. Railway mileage, none. Drained by the Tennessee and Hiwassee Rivers. Hiwassee River and valley lands are very fertile. Corn, wheat, oats, hay, and live stock are staple products. Decatur, the county seat, has a population of 142 and has a weekly newspaper, bank, and flourishing commercial establishments. Scholastic population of county 2,072; high schools, 1; elementary schools, 32.

MONROE COUNTY

MONROE COUNTY was erected in 1819 out of the Hiwassee Purchase and was named for President Monroe. At the time of the cession and for a long period of time previously the territory now in this county contained the old Indian towns of Chota, Tellico, Citico, and Toqua. Loudon was erected in 1756 at the junction of the Tellico and Little Tennessee Rivers. This was the first structure erected in Tennessee by Anglo-Americans.*

In 1825, at public sale of lands, the first sheriff, John McCrosky, and James Montgomery bought farms; and the son of the latter, M. J. C. Montgomery, was the first man in the United States to saw slanting fence posts.

Among the first settlers were: Samuel McSpadden, William Williams, William Ainsworth, Michael Carroll, William Bradley, James Axely, William Neal, Daniel Heiskell, Rev. Robert Sneed, Hugh H. Gregory, Alexander Biggs, Pressly Cleveland, Finley Gillespie, and Iredell Wright. Joseph B. Heiskell, who became Attorney-General of the State, studied law under Gillespie. Judge D. M. Key,† also, was born in this county.

The first court was held at Morganton (now in Loudon County). The next court was held at Henderson's, three miles east of Madisonville, the present county site, which was named for President Madison and was established probably in 1822, although some authorities say the site "was selected and a town platted in 1827."

*Ramsey's Annals of Tennessee, pages 51-53, 66, 85.
†Postmaster-General in President Hayes' cabinet.

Henderson and Johnson established in 1832, at Madisonville, an enterprise for the publication of "Dr. Gunn's Domestic Medicine," which enterprise attained somewhat large proportions for that day. It also published a few other books.

The enterprising town of Sweetwater had its beginning in 1852 in which year Newton Haun erected its first building.

The notable historical institutions of learning of the county are: Bolivar Academy, established following the compact of 1806; Hiwassee College, chartered in 1847, of which Dr. Robert Doak was the first president, from which many able men have gone forth; and Sweetwater College, of which the eminent Dr. J. L. Bachman was the head for more than twenty-five years. About twenty years ago it was converted into the Tennessee Military Academy, a large and flourishing institution.

Besides the notable men already mentioned, Monroe County has produced the following who have been or are now eminent in various lines of endeavor: Gideon Morgan, Gen. John C. Vaughn, who had a noteworthy record in the Confederate Army; John L. Hopkins, an attorney; Prof. S. G. Gilbreath, State Superintendent of Public Instruction under Governor Turney and now Superintendent of East Tennessee State Normal School at Johnson City; Dr. J. H. Brunner, for many years President of Hiwassee College.

Statistics of Monroe County: population, 1920, 22,060. Assessed valuation of taxable property, 1921, $11,916,448. Area, 580 square miles. Number of farms, 2,474. Railway mileage, 40. Monroe County joins North Carolina. Drained by Tellico and Little Tennessee Rivers. The eastern portion is mountainous and covered with valuable timber. The soil is fertile, the principal products being corn, wheat, potatoes, grasses, and live stock. The county has a good system of graded roads and a good mileage of hard surface roads. Iron ore, copper, barytes, and gold are found in the mountainous portions of the county. In the Coker Creek territory gold is found in places and quartz ledges and has been successfully mined, $80,000 having been taken off less than one acre. The Louisville & Nashville and the Southern Railway enter the county. Madisonville, the county seat, has a population of 850, is on the Atlantic Division of the L. & N. 45 miles from Knoxville, and has two banks, one weekly newspaper, flouring mills, lumber plant, good schools and churches. Sweetwater, on the Southern Railway, has a population of 1,972, one weekly newspaper, two banks, barytes mill, flour mill, planing mill, woolen mill, good schools and churches, and flourishing mercantile establishments. Tennessee Military Academy is located at Sweetwater. Tellico Plains has a population of 1,220, two banks, two lumber manufacturing plants, one tannic acid plant, roofing slate plant, and several stores. Scholastic population of county, 8,034; high schools, 4; elementary schools, 80.

MORGAN COUNTY

MORGAN COUNTY was erected in 1817 from Roane County and was named for Gen. Daniel Morgan. The first county site was at Montgomery. Later Wartburg was selected. It is said that the first settler was Samuel Hall, who located in 1807 about seven miles northeast of Wartburg. Other early comers were: Martin Hall, Joseph Stonecipher, Benjamin Stonecipher, Michael Stonecipher, Ezra Stonecipher, John M. Staples, Elijah Reese, Titus England, John Freels, Royal Price, William Shoemaker, Matthias Williams, Ephraim Davis, Morgan Hendricks, John Webb, Littleburg Brient, Lewis Rector, John Craig, and Basil Human.

Wartburg, the county seat, was settled by an enterprising and thrifty colony of Germans, who proved to be industrious and intelligent and did much for the material and educational interests of the county. The first term of the county court was held in January, 1818.

Morgan County contains great wealth in timber and coal, but most of the land suitable for cultivation is in the valleys.

The state possesses coal lands at Petros, the veins of which are worked by the convicts of the branch prison at that place.

That unique settlement called the Rugby Colony was established in the northwestern part of the county. Its first name was The Board of Aid to Land Ownership when it was organized by Boston people in 1877 and was changed three years later to Rugby Colony when the celebrated English author and other English capitalists became interested. Mr. Hughes opened the colony on October 5, 1880. They bought large tracts of land also in Scott and Fentress Counties.

Morgan County statistics: population, 1920, 13,285. Assessed valuation of taxable property, 1921, $7,724,137. Area, 448 square miles. Number of farms, 1,251. Railway mileage, 61. Drained by Emory and Obed Rivers. Its surface is hilly and well timbered with oak, chestnut, and pine. Corn, grasses, and live stock are staple products. Fruit growing is a paying industry. Large deposits of coal are found in the county. The Cincinnati Southern Railway intersects the county. Wartburg, the county seat, has a population of about

500, has a weekly newspaper, bank, and general stores. Scholastic population of county, 4,453; high schools, 4; elementary schools, 51.

POLK COUNTY

POLK COUNTY was created on November 28, 1839, from parts of McMinn and Bradley Counties and named for President (then Governor) James K. Polk. The county seat, "to be called Benton in honor of the Hon. Thomas H. Benton, a Senator in the Congress of the United States," was selected by vote of the people on February 8, 1840.

Settlements were made in 1836, the first town being Columbus, where the county court met on May 4, 1840. In August, 1840, the court met for the first time at Benton, which had been laid out on the McKamy farm. The Federal road from Knoxville to Cassville, Ga., passed through Polk County. Among the early settlers were: W. W. Biggs, Nelson Lawson, Abraham Lillard, Thomas Jones, R. W. McClary, Early Boyd, William Higgins, Michael Hildebrand, A. R. Stephenson, and John N. Taylor.

Ocoee Academy, a school for boys, was established at Benton, in 1844.

In mineral resources Polk is one of the richest counties in the state. In 1850 copper was discovered in the Ducktown basin, a low-grade copper, but of unknown depth and seemingly in inexhaustible quantities. Mixed with the ore is sulphur and, for years, the fumes thrown off in the process of reduction destroyed vegetation for many miles around and caused a suit to be entered by the State of Georgia against the State of Tennessee. Only a few years ago, however, the method of saving the sulphur fumes and, with them, producing sulphuric acid, a valuable byproduct has eliminated the former destruction of all vegetable growth. One of the most remarkable exhibits made by the State of Tennessee at the World's Fair at St. Louis was the copper ore furnished by the Tennessee Copper Company, which exhibit was secured for the state by Mr. A. P. Foster. The Ducktown Company is another very large corporation engaged in the production of copper. But copper, although the most valuable, is not the only mineral found in Polk County. No less than one hundred different minerals have been discovered in it, among them ten kinds of iron ore, gold, lead, graphite, lithograph stone, garnet, sulphur, granite, sandstone, quartz, manganese, limestone, talc, fluorspar, slate, and marble.

Statistics of Polk County: population, 1920, 14,247. Assessed valuation of taxable property, 1921, $16,883,592. Area, 400 square miles. Number of farms, 951. Railway mileage, 68. Drained by Hiwassee and Ocoee Rivers. The surface is mountainous and well timbered. Grazing for cattle and sheep is abundant. Extensive copper mines are operated in the county by the Ducktown Copper Company and the Tennessee Copper Company, the output being large. Lead is also found in the county, and there are large quarries of gray limestone. Corn, wheat, grass, and live stock are the principal products. The Louisville & Nashville Railroad traverses the county. Benton, the county seat, with a population of 525, is on the L. & N. three miles south of the Hiwassee River. It has good schools and churches, a weekly newspaper, bank, and general stores. Ducktown is the seat of the copper industry and has a population of 3,500. Copper Hill is another flourishing town. Scholastic population of county, 5,431; high schools, 3; elementary schools, 41.

RHEA COUNTY

RHEA COUNTY was erected on December 3, 1807, from Roane County and named for John Rhea,* a member of Congress from Sullivan County, Tenn., from 1803 to 1823. The Cherokees had relinquished their claim on the lands in the county by treaty in 1805.

In January, 1808, the first county court was organized at Big Springs, in the home of William Henry, about three or four miles north of Dayton. James Campbell was elected chairman; Daniel Rawlings, clerk; Miller Francis, sheriff; Thomas Woodward, coroner; Alex. Ferguson, register; Joseph Brooks, trustee; Thomas G. Brown, ranger; William Brown, solicitor. The justices at the time of the organization were: James Campbell, Jonathan Fine, Abraham Howard, John Henry, Joseph Brooks, Daniel Rawlings, and William Long.

On February 12, 1812, a committee, appointed to select the county seat, met at the home of Judge David Campbell and chose Washington at the head of Spring Creek. The site for the courthouse was on a grant of land owned by Richard G. Waterhouse, but Judge Campbell, having a claim upon a part of the grant, made a deed to the commissioners. The first

---

*It was John Rhea's testimony which exculpated Andrew Jackson in his controversy with the Monroe administration over his authority to enter Florida in the Seminole War.

courthouse was built in this year. The first circuit court was held in 1810.

Dayton, the present county seat, was previously Smith's Cross Roads and grew to a town of three thousand inhabitants in three years after a company of English capitalists, headed by Sir Titus Salts, located great iron furnaces in Rhea County in 1884.

Famous educational institutions of Rhea County are: Mars Hill School, afterwards changed to Tennessee Academy, Lorraine School, Tennessee Valley College, Dayton Masonic College, and Dayton University.

Early settlers were: James C. Mitchell, teacher of Hopkins L. Turney, father of Gov. Peter Turney; John Hackett, a famous land speculator; John Locke, cashier of the loan office of the old Bank of Tennessee; James Campbell, Robert Patterson, Jesse Roddye, David Murfree, and Daniel Walker.

Statistics of Rhea County: population, 1920, 13,812. Assessed valuation of taxable property, $8,947,220. Area, 360 square miles. Number of farms, 1,201. Railway mileage, 32. Drained by the Tennessee River. Surface partly mountainous. Cattle, corn, wheat, grass, and fruits are staple products. There has been remarkable development and advance in the cultivation of small fruits, a large annual business being done in the shipment of strawberries. This county is noted for its fine apples. Coal and iron ore are found in the county, and there are fine forests of marketable timber. The county is traversed by the Cincinnati Southern Railroad. Dayton, the county seat, has a population of 1,701. It is on the Cincinnati Southern Railroad 38 miles from Chattanooga. It is a flourishing town, with good business houses, churches, schools, weekly newspapers, banks, and several manufacturing establishments. Spring City and Grandview are flourishing towns with good schools. Scholastic population of county, 5,246; high schools, 4; elementary schools, 50.

ROANE COUNTY

ROANE COUNTY was erected November 6, 1801 and was formed from Knox County. It was named for Judge Roane, Governor, 1801-1803. After the Hiwassee Purchase, Roane County was extended on the south side of the Tennessee River and Morgan County was taken from it.

On November 30, 1793, a blockhouse was completed by John Sevier at Southwest Point, a station established in 1791, near Kingston, which was of great service to travelers and settlers as a protection against the Indians.

Capt. W. E. McElwee, of Rockwood, is authority for the following statement concerning the early history of this section: "In 1799 the Legislature then in session in Knoxville passed an act, 'To establish a town to be named Kingston, on the lands of Robert King, near Southwest Point, in Knox County, to be laid out under the direction of David Miller, Alexander Carmichael, George Preston, John Smith, William L. Lovely, and Thomas N. Clark. Later a petition was sent to the Assembly to create a new county, with Kingston for the county seat. This was done November 6, 1801. It was named in honor of Archibald Roane. There were in the county 275 men capable of bearing arms, organized into six companies. Only eight men were unable to sign their names to the muster rolls. Forty-two of them had been Revolutionary soldiers, among them being Captain Walker, who had commanded the body guard of Light Horse Harry Lee."

The road running from the Clinch River to the Cumberland settlements, built in 1785, passed through Roane County. When Knoxville became the capital of the Southwest Territory in 1792, the road was extended to that point. In 1822 it became a twice-a-week stage route, running through the main street of Kingston. At that time Kingston was a very important point. Its inns were stopping places for Jackson, Sevier, and other noted men of those days. On Monday, September 21, 1807, the Legislature met at Kingston, but adjourned to meet at Knoxville on Wednesday, September 23.

Early settlers were: Dr. Daniel Rather, Thomas C. Childress, Robert Allison, William French, David Patton, Thomas Brown, quartermaster for the garrison at Southwest Point, Gen. John Brown, owner of extensive lands, and William Brown, an eminent lawyer.

The Court of Pleas and Quarter Sessions was organized on December 20, 1801, at the home of Hugh Beatty, at which time the following magistrates were qualified: William White, Samuel Miller, Hugh Nelson, Paul Harlson, Zacheus Ayer, George Preston, William Campbell, James Preston, Isham Cox, William Barnett, George McPherson, and Abraham McClelland.

Early lawyers were: John Purvis, James McCampbell, W. C. Dunlap, J. W. Brazeale, J. Y. Smith, and I. Hope.

Soldiers from this county in the Creek War and the War of 1812 were: John Lloyd, Daniel Webster, Uriah Allison, Tom Margrave, and John Morrison. Sam Houston was a clerk in a store in Kingston when he enlisted as a soldier in the Creek War.

Rittenhouse Academy was one of the twenty-seven academies established in Tennesse in accordance with the terms of the compact of 1806. It educated many prominent men and women. For many years its principal was a Prussian of high birth, named H. W. von Aldehoff. He married a sister of Judge James Sevier, a grandson of John Sevier. Afterwards he established a celebrated school on Lookout Mountain and later moved to Dallas, Tex.

Statistics of Roane County: population, 1920, 24,624. Assessed valuation of taxable property, 1921, $14,239,897. Area, 450 square miles. Number of farms, 1,687. Railway mileage, 89. Drained by Tennessee River and tributaries. The surface is mountainous and covered with fine forests of timber. The soil is fertile in the valleys and river bottoms. Mineral resources are iron ore, coal, and building stone. Staple products are corn, wheat, grass, and live stock. Fine county for orchards and vineyards. The strawberry industry has been developed in the county. The county has a fine system of public highways. Kingston, the county seat, with a population of 516, is a flourishing town with good schools, churches, bank, and weekly newspaper. Harriman, with a population of 4,019, has fine schools and churches, banks, newspapers, and several manufacturing establishments. Rockwood, with a population of 4,652, is an iron and coke center and gives employment to a large number of people in these industries. It has fine schools and churches, banks, weekly newspaper, and manufacturing establishments. Scholastic population of county, 8,618; high schools, 5; elementary schools, 57.

SCOTT COUNTY

SCOTT COUNTY was erected on December 17, 1849, out of parts of Anderson, Campbell, Fentress, and Morgan Counties, and was named for Gen. W. S. Scott. It was surveyed by Sampson Stanfield. By the act creating it a Board of Commissioners was appointed consisting of William Titwood, W. W. Cotton, William Massengale, Drury Smith, John Tipton, William Rich, Thomas Lawson, William Carney, and J. W. Kerne. This Board appointed the following committee to locate the county seat: Isaac Reed, Bailey Buttram, James Litton, Riley Chambers, and Henry Massengale. They located the county seat at Huntsville, named in honor of a hunter of the early days whose name was Hunt.

The first election was held on March 2, 1850, and the following officers were elected: John Lewallen, Sheriff; Allen McDonald, County Court Clerk; John L. Smith, Circuit Court Clerk; Isaac Reed, Trustee; Riley Chambers, Registrar.

The first court was held in July, 1850, by Judge Alexander and Attorney-General David H. Cummings.

The first courthouse was erected in 1851 and was used until 1874, when a new courthouse was built. This, in turn, was superseded by the third which was built in 1906.

Statistics of Scott County: population, 1920, 13,411. Assessed valuation of taxable property, 1921, $7,170,922. Area, 620 square miles. Number of farms, 1,344. Railway mileage, 70. Drained by the tributaries of the Cumberland River. Surface is hilly and covered with fine forests. Staple products are corn, grass, and live stock. Considerable attention is given to the production of small fruits. Fine fire clay deposits are found. Huntsville, the county seat, with a population of about 500, has good schools, churches, a weekly newspaper, and flourishing business establishments. The chief town in the county is Oneida, on the Cincinnati Southern Railroad, with a population of 942. A railroad is being extended from Oneida into Fentress County. Helenwood is another flourishing town. Scholastic population of county, 5,411; high schools, 5; elementary schools, 61.

SEQUATCHIE COUNTY

SEQUATCHIE COUNTY was erected in 1857 out of Hamilton County and was named for Sequatchie Valley and Sequatchie River. It is traversed by the Sequatchie Valley which is very fertile. This county is rich in deposits of coal and iron. The county seat is Dunlap.

Statistics of Sequatchie County: population, 1920, 3,362. Assessed valuation of taxable property, 1921, $2,168,407. Area, 250 square miles. Number of farms, 339. Railway mileage, 14. Drained by the Sequatchie River and intersected by the Sequatchie Valley. Soil in the valleys is very fertile. One of the best grape-producing sections in the South. Fine hardwoods are found. Mineral resources are: limestone, coal, and iron ore. Corn, wheat, oats, grass, and live stock are staple products. Fine grazing lands for cattle. Traversed by the Nashville, Chattanooga & St. Louis Railway. Dunlap, the county seat, has a population of 1,465, and is a flourishing town with good schools, churches, business establishments, and a weekly newspaper. Scholastic population of county, 1,548; high schools, 1; elementary schools, 13.

SEVIER COUNTY

SEVIER COUNTY was erected by the Territorial Assembly on September 27, 1794, out of Jefferson County and was attached to the district of Hamilton. It was named for John Sevier, as was the county seat, Sevierville. The settlement of Sevier County began in 1783, when pioneers built a fort on Dumplin Creek and soon held a friendly conference with the Cherokee Indians. Maj. James Hubbard, whose family in Virginia had been murdered by the Shawnees, and who was an implacable enemy of all Indians, attended and attempted to intimidate the Cherokees. His efforts were thwarted by Capt. (afterwards General) James White.

Among the early settlers were: William Cannon, Jacob Huff, Samuel Blair, Allen Bryant, Peter Bryant, Joshua Gist (Judge of the Supreme Court of the State of Franklin), Thomas Bucking, who built the first brick house in the county eight miles south of Sevierville, and Isaac Thomas, a giant.

After the collapse of the State of Franklin, in 1788, the people who had been permitted by the Indians to locate in the region south of the French Broad River, which included what is now Sevier County, were ignored by the Governor of North Carolina. Being technically trespassers upon the lands of the Indians, in their emergency they set up a government of their own, which was the fourth independent government established in the State of Tennessee. This government continued until 1792 when Jefferson County was organized by Governor William Blount.

Sevierville was laid off in 1795. Only a few sessions of the court were held before the admission of the state into the Union. The first court after that event was held on July 4, 1796. The following magistrates were present: Samuel Newell, Joshua Gist, Joseph Wilson, Andrew Cowan, Joseph Vance, Robert Pollack, Peter Bryant, M. Lewis, John Clack, Robert Calvert, Adam Wilson, James Riggin, Alexander Montgomery, Jesse Griffin, Isom Green, James P. H. Porter, and Lewis Renan.

The first white child born in the county was Nancy Rogers, who married James P. H. Porter. Her name was bestowed on Nancy Academy, for the establishment of which the Legislature in 1813 authorized the holding of a lottery. George W. Pickle, State Attorney-General and reporter, was a resident of Sevierville in 1869.

Statistics of Sevier County: population, 1920, 22,384. Assessed valuation of taxable property, 1921, $8,840,827. Area, 560 square miles. Number of farms, 3,450. Railway mileage, 36. Drained by the French Broad River. Surface is mountainous and partly covered with fine timber. The soil in the valleys is rich and fertile. Fine limestone is quarried in the county. Staple products are: wheat, corn, grass, and live stock. Grazing for live stock is abundant. Sevierville, the count seat, with a population of 776, is on the Little Pigeon River and the Knoxville, Sevierville and Eastern Railroad, 30 miles from Knoxville. It has good schools, churches, two weekly newspapers, banks, and general stores and manufacturing establishments. Scholastic population of county, 8,503; high schools, none; elementary schools, 99.

SULLIVAN COUNTY*

SULLIVAN COUNTY, the second county formed in Tennessee, was created by the State of North Carolina in 1799, after a survey had shown that it was in this state and not in Virginia as had theretofore been thought. It was named for Gen. John Sullivan. With the exception of a small strip, Sullivan County was not, therefore, a part of Washington District when this district was created, but at that time was claimed by Virginia and was recognized as a part of that state.

Among the early settlers were John Rhea, Gen. George Rutledge, who commanded a company at King's Mountain, Gen. George Maxwell, Col. David Looney, and Richard Netherland, the Kings, Thomases, Dulaneys, Delaneys, Rutledges, Massengills, Snodgrasses, Snapps, Taylor, Senekers, Coxes, Bachmans, Bushongs, Andersons, Easleys, Cowans, Pyles, Bookers, Akards, Odells, Fains, Gaines, Rollers, and Crosses.

The claim is made by the people of Sullivan County that the first permanent settlements in what is now Tennessee were made by John and Thomas Sharpe in 1785, who located in the Holston Valley; and soon thereafter Joseph Martin, who had been with Dr. Thomas Walker on his early pathfinding expedition, made his home near Kingsport, and that Thomas

---

*A large part of the facts herein stated are taken from Historic Sullivan County by Oliver Taylor.

Henderson, John Womack, and the father of David Crockett came soon afterward.

In 1771, Evan and Isaac Shelby came, built a fort and opened a general store where the city of Bristol now stands, partly in Virginia and partly in Tennessee.

Near the present site of Kingsport was Fort Patrick Henry, named for the American patriot and orator, who was Governor of Virginia at the time. From this fort John Donelson and his fellow argonauts sailed on their long and perilous journey down the Tennessee River on December 22, 1779. Near here, too, was fought the battle of Island Flats on July 20, 1776, against the Cherokee Indians under Chief Dragging Canoe, in which the Indians were routed with severe loss. In this battle distinction was won by Capt. James Shelby, Lieut. Robert Davis, Robert Edminston, John Morrison, and Isaac Shelby. The last named, a volunteer, without authority gave an order which was obeyed and was the means of gaining the victory.

Early educational institutions were King's College at Bristol, Jefferson Academy and the Masonic Institute at Blountville. Dr. J. D. Tadlock was for many years the learned and beloved president of King's College. Among other leading educators may be mentioned: George Wilhelm, Archimedes Davis, J. H. Catron, Dr. A. J. Brown, Rev. T. F. Summers, Rev. John King, Rev. W. B. Gale, J. H. Seneker, William Daily, and James Snapp.

Among the brilliant legal lights should be given the following: William Blount, William Cocke, John Netherland, Matt Haynes, William Deaderick, C. J. St. John, and John Fain.

Statistics of Sullivan County: population, 1920, 36,259. Assessed valuation of taxable property, 1921, $25,577,079. Area, 410 square miles. Number of farms, 3,314. Railway mileage, 51. Drained by the Holston River and the head waters of the Tennessee River. Fine forests of timber. Soil is fertile. Fine deposits of iron ore, and limestone. Staple products are: fruits, wheat, corn, oats, grasses, live stock, poultry, eggs, and butter. Blountville, the county seat is nine miles southwest of Bristol and has a population of about 400, and it has good schools and churches, bank and flourishing business establishments. Bristol is in a center of a territory rich in mineral deposits. The Tennessee section of the city has a population of 8,047 and is 131 miles from Knoxville. It is an up-to-date city with all modern conveniences. Five railroads enter the city, including the Southern and the Norfolk & Western. Bristol has large lumber interests, a large tannery, and a large number of manufacturing establishments. A large iron furnace is located here. The city has daily and weekly newspapers, fine schools and churches, good hotels and mercantile establishments. Kingsport, with a population of 5,692, is a new industrial town in Sullivan County. It is only a few years old, and before and during the World War it employed several thousand in the various industries, which include a dye plant, cement plant, brick-making plant, a printing plant, and several other industries. During the war some of the plants were used in the manufacture of munitions. Some of the plants are now closed down. Scholastic population of county, 11,463; high schools, 6; elementary schools, 77.

UNICOI COUNTY

UNICOI COUNTY was erected on March 19, 1875, out of Washington and Carter Counties and was named for the Unicoi Mountain. The name "Unicoi" means white. Section 16 of the Act creating this county says: "That for the purpose of organizing the county of Unicoi, William Tillson, Esq., Charles Bean, Josiah Sams, James V. Johnson, William McInterf, David Bell, Franklin Hannum, Richard N. Morris, and Thomas Wright shall be, and they are hereby appointed commissioners on the part of the several fractions in which they reside."

Unicoi County was attached to the first judicial court.

The first county court was organized on January 3, 1876, with the following-named magistrates present: Henry McKinney, A. E. Briggs, D. T. O'Brian, B. W. Woodward, M. C. Burchfield, Isaac Gilbert, Alexander McInturf, G. E. Tompkins, James M. Norris, R. B. Hensley, R. L. Rowe, Alexander Masters, J. M. Anderson, William Parks, G. Garland, J. S. Yader, William McInturf, and Baptist McNabb.

The county seat was first named Vanderbilt, which name was retained until 1879 when it was changed by the Legislature to Ervin. By an error the post office department of the government spelled it Erwin, which spelling it still retains.

Early settlers were: Jesse Brown, Enoch Job, Richard Deakins, George Martin, William Lewis, James Acton, Jonathan Webb, Robert Hampton. In the early days, like most of the early pioneers of East Tennessee, they suffered much from the Indians. The first church was Baptist, established probably in 1785.

Unicoi County is rich in timber and mineral resources.

Statistics of Unicoi County: population, 1920, 10,120. Assessed valuation of taxable property, 1921, $4,590,561. Area, 196 square miles. Number of farms, 811. Railway mileage, 21. Drained by the Nollichucky River and intersected by Carolina, Clinchfield & Ohio Railway. Surface is mountainous. Cotton, corn, oats, grasses, and live stock are the staple products. Erwin, the county seat, with a population of 2,965, is 15 miles south of Johnson City and is a flourishing manufacturing town, one of the principal industries being the production of chinaware. Erwin has good schools, churches, a weekly newspaper and flourishing business establishments. Scholastic population of county, 3,163; high school, 1; elementary schools, 33.

UNION COUNTY

UNION COUNTY was erected on January 3, 1850, out of Grainger, Claiborne, Campbell, Anderson, and Knox Counties, and the following-named men were appointed commissioners who organized the county: William T. Carden, John F. Huddleston, Ezra Buckner, and William Colvin, of Grainger County; Malcijah Nash, J. G. Palmer, and John Sharpe, of Claiborne County; Isaac C. Meril Hill and Hazell Hill, of Campbell County; James W. Turner, Allen M. Coy, and A. L. Carden of Anderson County; Henry Graves and Henry G. Roberts, of Knox County.

But the organization of the county was delayed, for the people of Knox County, not relishing the loss of that part of the county which was to be taken into the new county, entered suit and secured an injunction against its acting as a county. Horace Maynard, who at that time was a member of Congress from the First Tennessee District, which embraced the proposed new county, defended the suit for Union County in prolonged litigation which was finally decided in favor of Union County in 1853.

Because of the valuable services rendered by Mr. Maynard in this litigation, the county seat was named Maynardsville. The first county court was organized there on February 6, 1854, with the following-named magistrates present: Elijah Evans, John Lowry, William Calvin, G. B. Carden, William Needham, J. G. Palmer, Jacob Turner, Calvin B. Howard, and Enoch Branson. Complete organization of the county was effected in 1856.

This county is rich in deposits of iron ore, marble, lead, and zinc.

Statistics of Union County: Population, 1920, 11,615. Assessed valuation of taxable property, 1921, $3,877,437. Area, 220 square miles. Number of farms, 2, 060. Railway mileage, 7. Drained by the Clinch and Powell Rivers. Surface is mountainous and partly covered with fine timber. Fine deposits of iron, zinc, lead and marble are found in the county. Corn, oats, wheat, live stock and dairy products are staple. Maynardsville, the county seat, has a population of about 500 and has good schools, churches, banks, and flourishing business establishments. Scholastic population of county, 4,187; high schools, 6; elementary schools, 49.

WASHINGTON COUNTY

WASHINGTON COUNTY was erected* by the General Assembly of North Carolina in November, 1777.

It was formed from Washington District which had been detached from Wilkes and Burke Counties and included all the present State of Tennessee, although a part of it, was thought at the time to belong to Virginia. This county has the distinction of being the first political division in the United States which was named in honor of George Washington. From it all the other counties in Tennessee have been carved. It is, therefore, the oldest county in the state and was the theatre of the important events which occurred in its early history.

At this session of the Legislature provision was also made for opening a land office in Washington County, permission being given that each head of a family might take up six hundred and forty acres, his wife and his children one hundred acres each, all at the rate of forty shillings per hundred acres. The facility with which settlers might obtain lands caused a large influx of pioneers immediately, although no wagon road had been opened across the mountains.

At least eight years prior to the formation of this county permanent settlers had taken up their abodes on the Watauga, as we have seen. The Watauga Association was formed in 1772, and Henderson's Purchase of the Transylvania Country was made from the Indians by treaty signed in 1775 on the Watauga.

John Carter, who had been chairman of the court of the Watauga Association, was appointed colonel of Washington County.

*Chapter XXXI of the Laws of N. C., Iredell's Revisal, page 346. By this act the County of Washington was "declared to be part of the District of Salisbury."

Counties of Tennessee

The county was organized on February 23, 1778, with the following-named magistrates in attendance: John Carter, chairman, John Sevier, Jacob Womack, Robert Lucas, Andrew Greer, John Shelby, George Russell, William Been, Zachariah Isbell, John McNabb, Thomas Houghton, William Clark, John McMahan, Benjamin Gist, John Chisholm, Joseph Willson, William Cobb, James Stuart, Michael Woods, Richard White, Benjamin Wilson, James Robertson, and Valentine Sevier. On the next day the officers were elected as follows: John Sevier, clerk; Valentine Sevier, sheriff; James Stuart, surveyor; John Carter, entry-taker; John McMahan, register; Jacob Womack, stray-master; John McNabb, coroner.

The first courthouse was built by Charles Robertson. Andrew Jackson lived in Jonesboro when he first came to Tennessee and boarded with a Mr. Chester.

Jonesboro, the oldest town in the state, was selected for the county seat. It was named for Willie (pronounced Wylie) Jones, who had shown himself friendly to the Watauga settlers when they had sent delegates to Halifax, N. C., to see the governor. Jonesboro was laid off in 1779. The first and the last Legislatures of the State of Franklin met at Jonesboro. Many noted men have lived in this historic place. Among them were: David Nelson, author of "The Cause and Cure of Infidelity"; B. F. Lundy, publisher of an abolition paper; W. G. Brownlow, before he moved to Knoxville; Landon C. Haynes, uncle of Robert L. and Alfred A. Taylor; Judge T. A. R. Nelson; and Chief Justice J. W. Deaderick.

Statistics of Washington County: population, 1920, 34,052. Assessed valuation of taxable property, 1921, $24,687,316. Area, 344 square miles. Number of farms, 2,865. Railway mileage, 59. Drained by the Nollichucky, Watauga, and Holston Rivers. Surface is diversified with mountains and valleys, with forests of fine timber. Mineral resources, iron ore and building stone. Intersected by the Southern Railway, and other railways are the Carolina, Clinchfield and Ohio and the East Tennessee & Western North Carolina. Jonesboro, the county seat, has a population of 815, is on the Southern Railway and has fine schools, churches, newspaper, banks, iron foundry, and several manufacturing establishments. Johnson City has a population of 12,442 and has a large number of manufacturing establishments. It is the seat of the National Soldiers' Home and the East Tennessee Normal. It has daily and weekly newspapers and is one of the flourishing cities in East Tennessee. Scholastic population of county 10,247; high schools, 10; elementary schools, 60.

MIDDLE TENNESSEE

BEDFORD COUNTY

BEDFORD COUNTY was erected on December 3, 1807, out of Rutherford County and was named for Thomas Bedford. It was organized in 1808. Early settlers were: Clement Cannon, Philip Burrow, Freeman Burrow, William McMahon, Matt Martin, Barkley Martin, Mrs. Mary Scruggs, William Hix, Robert and Henry Hastings, "Sally" Sailors, Joseph Tillman, James Reagan, David Floyd, Thomas Gibson, and Cuthbert Word. The two Martins and five of their brothers served seven years under George Washington.

Several thousand acres of land in Bedford County were issued by North Carolina to the officers and soldiers of the Continental Line. Others were issued for the State of Tennesee. Among the latter was a grant to Andrew Jackson for land near Fall Creek.

In 1808 the county was organized at the home of Mrs. Payne near the head of Mulberry Creek. In 1809 the Legislature passed an act providing for the appointment of a committee consisting of John Atkinson, William Wood, Barthell Martin, Howell Dandy, and David McKissack to locate a county site within two miles of the center of the county. Afterwards, John Lane and Benjamin Bradford were added to the committee. The home of Amos Balch, two or three miles southeast of Shelbyville, was the county seat temporarily. It was permanently located at Shelbyville* in May, 1810, on land donated by Clement Cannon. Shelbyville was incorporated on October 7, 1819.

The first courthouse was erected in 1810 or soon afterwards. The first chancery court was held in 1836. Prominent lawyers of the early days were: Archibald Yell, who was governor of Arkansas, 1840-1844, William Gilchrist, I. J. Frierson, William H. Wisener, Henry Cooper, Hugh L. Davidson, and Thomas Whitesides.

Early physicians were: Doctors J. G. Barksdale, Grant Whitney, James Kincade, Frank Blakemore, G. W. Fogleman, and John Blakemore.

Famous schools were: Salem Academy, established at Bellbuckle in 1820; the Martin School at Fairfield, in 1828; the school of Rev. George Newton, started near Wartrace in 1815 or 1816; Dixon Academy, established in Shelbyville in 1820;

---

*Named for Col. Isaac Shelby.

the Webb School at Bellbuckle; the Brandon Training School at Wartrace; and the Tate School at Shelbyville.

Probably the earliest church was Salem, built about 1807 near Shelbyville. Rev. John Brooks "rode circuit" in this county.

The war record of Bedford County is remarkable. It furnished a full company in the War of 1812, which took part in the battle of New Orleans. Its captain was Barrett, and some of the members were: John Farrer, William Hazlett, James Gowan, Michael Womack, John L. Neil, James, Philip, and William Burrows, John Casteel, William Wood, "Sally" Sailors, Robert Fergison, William P. Finch, John Pool, Andrew Mathus, Townsend Fugett, Wesley Rainwater, Benjamin Webb, Martin Hancock, J. L. Dillard, John Murphey, Moses Pruitt, and James Scott. It furnished a full company under Captain Hunter in the second Seminole War. In this company were: Lewis Tillman, William Wood, Albert Smell, John Hudlow, John Stone, Standards, Thomas, and Abraham McMahon. In the War with Mexico it furnished a company under Capt. E. W. Frierson. In the War between the States it furnished troops to both the Federal and the Confederate Armies in almost equal proportions.

Statistics of Bedford County: population, 1920, 21,737. Assessed valuation of taxable property, 1921, $17,532,014. Area, 550 square miles. Number of farms, 3,340. Railway mileage, 25. Drained by Duck River and tributaries. Traversed by Nashville, Chattanooga & St. Louis Railway. Farms are in a fine state of cultivation, and staple products are: corn, wheat, cotton, grasses, and live stock. Shelbyville, the county seat, has a population of 2,912, and is on a branch of the N. C. & St. L. Railway. It has an electric light plant, water works, cotton factory, a hub and spoke factory, foundry, saw mills, planing mills, and other manufacturing enterprises, with good banks, churches, schools, and two newspapers. Other prosperous towns are: Bellbuckle, Wartrace, Normandy, Flat Creek, and Unionville. Scholastic population of county, 7,403; high schools, 5; elementary schools 74.

CANNON COUNTY

CANNON COUNTY was erected on January 21, 1836, out of Warren, Coffee, Wilson, and Rutherford Counties and was named for Newton Cannon, who was Governor at that time and who appointed a commission of five members to established the lines between Cannon and the adjoining counties and to lay off a public square at Danville, which was the name of the county seat until it was changed to Woodbury in honor of Gen. Levi Woodbury.

Henry D. McBroom and his brother owned most of the land on and adjacent to the public square of Woodbury and the former gave every alternate lot around it to those who would put up a structure on it. He also owned the only hotel or inn at that time. He later built the Dillon Hotel, which was a historic structure. It was burned in 1907.

At the time the county was organized the only store in Woodbury (Danville) was that of Henry Wiley.

Among the early pioneers were: Henry D. McBroom, William Hollis, John Wood, Henry Ford, William Mears, Usibel Stone, Benjamin Allen, George St. John, William McFerrin, Joshua Barton, Archibald Stone, Asa Smith, Elijah Stephens, William Preston, Sr., Walter Wood, Benjamin Cummings, Sr., Warren Cummings, William Cummings, Sr., John Stone, Andrew Melton, Alexander McBroom, William James, John Wood, James Todd, Benjamin Hale, John Haley, Archibald Hicks, Gideon Rucker, Lonis Jetton, Gabriel Elkins, James Avent, and Lemuel Moore.

The first county court met in May, 1836, at the tavern of Henry D. McBroom, with the following-named magistrates in attendance: Thomas Powell, Allen Haley, Joseph Simpson, Blake Sedgley, Isaac Finley, James L. Essary, Isaac W. Ellidge, John Pendleton, I. M. Brown, Elijah Stephens, F. L. Turner, C. C. Evans, John Melton, Samuel Lance, William Bates. John Martin, William B. Foster, John Frazer, Martin Phillips, Lemuel Moore, Reuben Evans, James Goodwin, Peter Reynolds, James Batey, Joel Cheatham, and Jonathan Fuston. The following-named officials qualified at this meeting: Samuel J. Garrison, county court clerk; George Grizzle, sheriff; Alexander F. McFerrin, register; Job Stephens, trustee; Alexander McKnight, coroner; Henry H. Clifton, ranger; William Stone, entry-taker; Hugh Robinson, surveyor. A committee of six, consisting of Hugh Robinson, James Clark, Arch Stone, William Bates, John B. Stone, and John Brown, was appointed to lay off town lots.

Statistics of Cannon County: population, 1920, 10,241. Assessed valuation of taxable property, 1921, $4,248,639. Area, 280 square miles. Number of farms, 1,992. Railway mileage, none. Drained by numerous small streams. Surface is hilly and rolling and soil very fertile. Corn, wheat, and live stock are staple products. Woodbury, the county seat, has a population of 277 and is a flourishing town with good schools, churches, bank, weekly newspaper, and prosperous mercantile establishments. Scholastic population of county, 4,560; high schools, 7; elementary schools, 34.

CHEATHAM COUNTY

CHEATHAM COUNTY was erected on February 28, 1856, out of parts of Davidson, Robertson, Dickson, and Montgomery Counties and was named in honor of Nathaniel Cheatham, Speaker of the Senate at this time. Early settlers located along the streams. Benjamin Darrow located his home near Sycamore Mills about 1790. About the same time John Hyde and Howard Alley settled near Pleasant View. In 1796 a settlement was made at Ashland City by Robert Heaton and Braxton Lee. For the protection of the settlers against the Indians a block house was erected at Half Pone.

The first county court was held at Sycamore Mills on May 15, 1856, when the following magistrates qualified: W. L. Gower, chairman, B. F. Binkley, J. M. Lee, E. L. Hooper, Jesse Hooper, N. Crockett, J. L. Majors, R. T. Gupton, W. W. Williams, A. J. Bright, and R. L. Weakley. Samuel Watson, the first county judge, qualified on the first Monday in June, 1856. For the county seat, land was bought at Ashland from Mr. Lennox. The county court held its sessions at Forest Hill, a short distance south of Ashland until November, 1857, when its session was held for the first time at Ashland.

On December 8, 1859, Ashland became an incorporated town under the name of Ashland City, but through negligence of county officials the charter was forfeited. It was incorporated again with E. Dozier as mayor about fourteen years ago.

To Prof. A. S. Link is due, in no small degree, the great interest which the people of this county take in education. He founded Ashland Institute in 1880, and after one year was joined by R. S. Turner. Professor Link also established the Link School at Thomasville in 1902. In 1859 Millwood Academy was opened at Sycamore by Professors Marvin and Lawrence. In 1884 Pleasant View School was opened by Prof. W. I. Harper. In 1868 the Sycamore Powder Mills bought the entire machinery of the Confederate works at Augusta, Ga., and moved it to Sycamore, where it produced an important output until 1904.

At the narrows of the Harpeth River, Montgomery Bell carried on the manufacture of iron for many years.

Statistics of Cheatham County: population, 1920, 10,039. Assessed valuation of taxable property, 1921, $4,840,766. Area,

400 square miles. Number of farms, 1,449. Mileage of railway, 28. Drained by Cumberland River and its tributaries. Surface is rolling and generally fertile. Has a fine growth of timber. Corn, tobacco, wheat, and live stock are staple products. The Nashville, Chattanooga & St. Louis Railway and the Tennessee Central Railway traverse the county. Ashland City, the county seat, has a population of 649, is on the Cumberland River and the Tennessee Central Railway, and has good schools, churches, a bank, newspapers, and several prosperous business establishments. Scholastic population of county, 3,413; high schools, 3; elementary schools, 58.

CLAY COUNTY

CLAY COUNTY was named in honor of Henry Clay. It was erected December 7, 1870, from nearly equal parts of Jackson and Overton Counties. Celina was selected for the county seat over Butler's Landing and Bennett's Ferry. Celina is located at the mouth of Obed River and for many years has been one of the most important trading and shipping points on the upper Cumberland.

In that part of Clay County taken from Overton County, and in Overton County, John Sevier located 57,000 acres of land of the visit to which he refers in his diary, a copy of which was secured by the Tennessee Historical Society only a few years ago. After his death, in 1815, his widow moved to the Dale, known later as the Clark Place in Clay County. From there she moved to Alabama where she died. Her remains were removed to Knoxville last year and now repose beside those of her distinguished husband.

Statistics of Clay County: population, 1920, 9,193. Assessed valuation of taxable property, 1921, $3,571,848. Area, 217 square miles. Number of farms, 1,605. Railway mileage, none. This county borders on Kentucky and is drained by the Cumberland River and its tributary, Obed River. Its surface is hilly, and the soil of the river bottoms is very fertile. It has fine forests of timber. Corn, tobacco, wheat, oats, and live stock are staple products. Celina, the county seat, has a population of 420. It is on the Cumberland River and has good schools, churches, a bank, a weekly newspaper, and a number of prosperous mercantile establishments. Scholastic population of county, 3,077; high schools, 4; elementary schools, 45.

COFFEE COUNTY

COFFEE COUNTY was organized on May 2, 1846, and was originally composed of Warren, Franklin, and Bedford Counties. It was named in honor of Gen John Coffee. By act of the Legislature, passed on January 8, 1836, the following named commissioners were appointed to run the boundary lines of the new county and to locate the county seat: Hugh Davidson, Alexander Blakely, David Hickerson, Thomas Powers, William Bradshaw, and Lecil Bobo. They selected a site on the lands of James Evans and Andrew Haynes, who, on March 1, 1836, donated two hundred acres to the county for this purpose. In March, 1836, also, the following-named men were elected magistrates from the ten civil districts into which the county had been divided: Adam Rayburn, John G. Walker, Alfred Ashley, John Lusk, Larkin Burham, Robert S. Rayburn, Alexander Downey, James Yell, Gabriel Jones, William Hodge, Johnson Garrett, Josiah Berry, John Charles, William Montgomery, Wade Stroud, Lecil Bobo, John W. Camden, Jesse Wooten, James M. Arnold, and William Holmes.

Their first session was on May 2, 1836, at the Baptist meeting house on the site of Manchester. John W. Camden was made chairman and the following officers qualified: Daniel McLean, county court clerk; John Bell, sheriff; James A. Brantley, register; Moses F. White, trustee; William P. Harris, coroner.

The sessions of the county court were held in the log house used by the Baptists as a church until 1837, when a courthouse was erected.

The circuit court was organized in June, 1836, with Samuel Anderson as a judge and James Whiteside as attorney-general. Its sessions were held in the log house of a private citizen.

It is said that Manchester, the county seat, was named for Manchester, England, because it was thought that the Coffee County capitol would, in time, be famed like its imagined prototype, for its iron manufactures.

Near Manchester, in the forks of Duck River, is what is known as Stone Fort, evidently a fortification of some prehistoric race. It encloses an area of thirty-seven acres, and from its walls of loose stones covered with earth have grown trees of great age.

Statistics of Coffee County: population, 1920, 17,344. Assessed valuation of taxable property, 1921, $9,405,734. Area, about 350 square miles. Number of farms, 2,314. Railway mileage, 29. This county is situated at the western base of the Cumberland Mountains and is traversed by the Nashville, Chattanooga & St. Louis Railway. The soil is a mixture of loam and sand, with a good clay subsoil, and is easily worked. Fruits and vegetables can be produced in great abundance. Tobacco cultivation is becoming extensive. Staple products are wheat, corn, oats, tobacco, and live stock. The county is drained by Duck River and its tributaries. Manchester, the county seat, has a population of 1,114, is on the north fork of Duck River and on the N. C. & St. L. Railway. It has churches, schools, banks, two weekly newspapers, waterworks, and many prosperous business establishments. Tullahoma, on the main line of the N. C. & St. L. Railway, has a population of 3,479, has fine schools, churches, banks, a weekly newspaper, an electric light plant, and numerous manufacturing establishments and prosperous stores. Scholastic population of county, 5,812; high schools, 3; elementary schools, 61.

DAVIDSON COUNTY

DAVIDSON COUNTY was created by an act of the Legislature of North Carolina, approved October 6, 1783. It originally included most of the territory west of the Cumberland Mountains now included in Middle Tennessee. It was named for Gen. William Lea Davidson, concerning whom Mr. Hugh Davidson, of Shelbyville, says: "Gen. William Lea Davidson was killed at Cowan's Ford, N. C., February 1, 1781, while resisting the advance of British troops commanded by Colonel Hall. Davidson County, N. C., Davidson College, Davidsonville, and Davidson River were named in his honor. Also, Davidson County, Tenn., and Davidson Academy. His widow, who was Miss Mary Brevard, a daughter of John Brevard, came with her family at a very early date near Nashville and experienced the dangers and privations of pioneer life.

"It was believed by General Davidson's friends and relations in North Carolina that he was killed by a renegade Tory, Frederick Hager, as his body was pierced by a bullet from what was considered a small bored gun at that time and Hager was known to carry that gun at that time. After the Revolutionary War, Hager, together with several others of his renegade class, fled to Tennessee. About 1811, John Davidson and Hugh Davidson came out from Buncombe County, N. C. The first settled on "Union Ridge" and the latter about two miles up Duck River from Normandy. Hager, hearing of these two

Davidsons, fled again, this time to the wilderness of Arkansas, to a point on the Arkansas River now known as Six Post, where he finished his miserable existence, leaving a large family.

"Gen. William Lea Davidson was a first cousin of Maj. William Davidson, 4th N. C. Reg. Cont. Line. From Maj. William Davidson descend the Davidson family and the Hons. George N. and Abram Tillman, of Nashville."

When Davidson county was formed, the county seat was named Nashborough, after Gen. Francis Nash, of North Carolina, who was killed in the battle of Germantown. The name was changed to Nashville by act of the North Carolina Legislature in 1784. In this year the first courthouse was built of hewn logs, was eighteen feet square with a lean-to of twelve feet.

Statistics of Davidson County: population, 1920, 167,815. Assessed valuation of taxable property, 1921, 197,134,968. Area, 508 square miles. Number of farms, 3,051. Railway mileage, 150. Drained by the Cumberland River and its tributaries. Its surface is gently undulating and in some sections is well timbered. Soil is fertile and well adapted to diversified agriculture. The county successfully produces 67 different field crops and 54 varieties of garden vegetables. Ten varieties of berries are grown in the county, and more than a dozen varieties of other fruits. The county has a fine system of free turnpikes. Staple products are: corn, wheat, cotton, oats, grass, fruits, and live stock. Dairying industry has increased largely in the last few years. Nashville, the county seat and capital of the state, has a population of 118,342. It is situated on the Cumberland River, which is navigable below Nashville to the Ohio and above Nashville to Point Burnside, Ky., a distance of about 350 miles, during a part of the year. Government locks and dams make the river navigable for all the year as far as Carthage, and it is expected that the system will be completed to Point Burnside. Besides the river, Nashville has excellent transportation facilities in the Louisville & Nashville Railway, the Nashville, Chattanooga & St. Louis Railway, and the Tennessee Central Railway. The city has splendid streets and owns its own electric light and water plants. The city has nearly 100 miles of electric railway and two interurban lines reaching towns in adjoining counties. Nashville is one of the largest jobbing centers in the South, supplying a large territory in Tennessee and adjoining states. It is a large manufacturing center, its industries giving employment to many thousands of wage earners. It is one of the largest hardwood lumber markets in the United States, and its milling interests are larger than those of any other Southern city. It is a large boot and shoe market and engages largely in the manufacture of these articles. Its daily newspapers have wide circulations and large influence. Its book and periodical business is the largest of any city in the South, and it is the second largest religious publication center in the United States. It is a financial center, its banks having combined assets of $60,000,000. Clearings for 1921 amounted to $845,509,813.12. Its public schools are as good as those of any city in the country, and its other institutions of learning, including Vanderbilt University, Peabody College for Teachers, and Ward-Belmont College for young women have made it famous in all the branches of learning. Information will be furnished by the Chamber of Commerce of Nashville. Scholastic population of county, 50,835; high schools, 17; elementary schools 86.

DeKALB COUNTY

DeKALB COUNTY was erected in 1837 out of parts of White, Warren, Cannon, Wilson, and Jackson Counties and was named for Baron DeKalb, an officer in the Revolutionary War who had fallen at Camden, New Jersey. The act creating this county provided that the first court should be held at the house of Bernard Richardson, near Smithville, which was chosen for the county seat and named for John Smith Bryan, who was commonly called "Smith." The committee appointed to select the county seat was: Thomas Durham, Joseph Banks, Thomas Allen, Watson Cantrell, and Joseph Clark.

Bernard Richardson gave to the county fifty acres for the county seat, a part of which was laid out in lots which were sold at public sale.

On March 5, 1838, the county was organized with the following-named magistrates in attendance: Lemuel Moore, chairman, Reuben Evans, Joseph Turney, Thomas Simpson, John Martin, Watson Cantrell, David Fisher, William Scott, Samuel Strong, Henry Burton, Martin Phillips, John Frazier, Joel Cheatham, Jonathan Fuston, Peter Reynolds, and James Batey.

A. J. Marchbanks was the first circuit judge and B. L. Ridley the first chancellor.

The first settlement in DeKalb County was made in 1797 by Adam Dale, who came from Maryland and located on

Smith's Fork Creek near Liberty and erected there the first mill in the county.

Other early settlers were: Thomas Whaley, Josiah Duncan, Henry Burton, Thomas West, William and John Dale, James and William Bratton, William and George Givan, the Walkers, the Pruitts, Jacob and Abraham Overall, Robin Forester, Reuben Evan, Matthew Sellers, Benjamin Blades, Nicholas Smith, Benjamin Garrison, Jesse Allen, Martin Phillips, Brition Johnson, Giles Driver, Levi Bozarth, David Taylor, P. G. Magness, Zachariah Lefever, John Wooldridge, Bernard Richardson, William Adcock, Wm. Floyd, John Vantrease, Jonathan and Stewart Doss, E. Turner, James Goodner, Edmund Turner, William Grandstaff, Thomas Simpson, and William Wright.

Statistics of DeKalb County: population, 1920, 15,370. Assessed valuation of taxable property, 1921, $7,497,060. Area, 310 square miles. Number of farms, 2, 792. Railway mileage, none. Drained by the Caney Fork River. Surface is hilly in part and well covered with timber. The soil is fertile and the stable products are corn, wheat, and live stock. Splendid fruit-growing section. Has some deposits of zinc and clay. Smithville, the county seat, has a population of 687, good schools and churches, a weekly newspaper, bank, flourishing stores, flour mill, and spoke and handle factory. Alexandria has a population of 510, has good schools and churches, bank and prosperous business establishments. Liberty is another thriving town in DeKalb County. Scholastic population of county, 4,728; high schools, 5; elementary schools, 71.

DICKSON COUNTY

DICKSON COUNTY was erected on October 3, 1803, out of part of Robertson and part of Montgomery Counties and was named for William Dickson, a member of Congress, representing the Mero District. Its first settlements began about 1793 when a large body of land was granted by the State of North Carolina to Robert Bell and described as being located on Jones Creek. In February of the same year the Cumberland Furnace, the earliest furnace in the West, was started by James Robertson, by whom it was sold to Montgomery Bell. All deeds were proven before Andrew Jackson, one of the judges of the Superior Court of Law and Equity.

The first county and circuit courts were held at the home of James Nesbit, on Barton's Creek, a few miles from Charlotte. It was organized by the following-named magistrates:

Montgomery Bell, William Doak, Sterling Brewer, William Russell, Gabriel Allen, William Teas, Samuel Harvey, Richard Napier, and Jesse Croft.

In 1804 the town of Charlotte, named for Aunt Charlotte Robertson, one of the early settlers, was laid off by a man named Ash, who reserved the central lot for a courthouse. In 1806 it became the county seat. Tracy Academy, a noted educational institution, was established there about 1830. Between 1810 and 1812 the county buildings were completed, and for the next twenty or twenty-five years Charlotte was a place of much importance. From 1819 to 1821 the supreme court held regular sessions there.

Early settlers in this county were: John Nesbitt, Montgomery Bell, Richard Napier, Abraham Caldwell, and Hudson Johnson.

On May 12, 1810, the Cumberland Presbyterian Church was organized at the home of Rev. Samuel McAdoo, near the present city of Dickson, and its centennial celebration was fittingly observed in 1910.

In consequence of the effort made, fifteen or twenty years ago, to move the county seat from Charlotte to Dickson, the county now has a courthouse at each of these towns and two circuits and chancery courts, an arrangement which has proved eminently satisfactory.

In 1897 an effort was made to establish a Socialist Colony in this county, which effort attracted nation-wide attention. J. A. Wayland, of Greencastle, Ind., located a company at Tennessee City and established there a periodical entitled "The Coming Nation." Dissension arose and Wayland went away, but those of the colony who remained secured a site on Yellow Creek at the noted Adam's Cave, six miles north of Tennessee City, where, under new leadership, they began operating again, continued the publication of "The Coming Nation," and named the enterprise The Ruskin Colony. Dissensions, however, again arose, a legal battle ensued and the effort ended in disaster. The remnant of the colony removed to Waycross, Ga. Ruskin Cave and the site of the former colony are now the property of the Ruskin Cave College Company.

Statistics of Dickson County: population, 1920, 19,342. Assessed valuation of taxable property, 1921, $7,617,329. Area, 620 square miles. Number of farms, 2,544. Railway mileage, 49. Drained by the Cumberland River and its tributary, Harpeth River. Surface undulating, partly covered with forest. Soil is fertile and the staple products are corn, wheat, tobacco, and live stock. Charlotte, the county seat, has a population of 200, is 12 miles from the N. C. & St. L. Railway and has good schools and churches, a bank and flourishing stores. Dickson, on the N. C. & St. L. Railway, is a town of 2,263 population and has excellent schools, churches, a weekly newspaper, manufacturing establishments, banks, and stores doing large business. Scholastic population of county, 6,488; high schools, 4; elementary schools, 79.

FENTRESS COUNTY

FENTRESS COUNTY was erected in 1823 out of Overton and Morgan Counties and was named for James Fentress, Speaker of the House of Representatives for five consecutive terms, from 1814-1823. Jamestown, the county seat, was named for his praenomen. Before this action it was called Sand Springs. In 1827, John M. Clemens, father of Samuel Clemens (Mark Twain) was a lawyer residing in Jamestown and the Obedstown of the "Gilded Age" was the Jamestown of that time, now familiarly known as Jimtown.

The first court was held at Three Forks of the Wolf's River. The first courthouse* was built in 1828 and Jamestown was incorporated in 1837.

Among the first settlers were: Conrad Pile, Pearson Miller, Arthur Frogge, John Riley, and Moses Poor.

Obey's River, or Obed River, is said to have been named for one of the long hunters, Obadiah Terrill.

This county was the home of the notorious Federal bushwhacker, "Tinker Dave" Beattie, and of Calvin Logston, who, with others, perpetrated cruel and bloody deeds in reconstruction times, and also of Marsha Millsaps, who, in 1843, was charged with being a witch, and of "Old Man" Stout who, in 1835, was accused of practicing witchcraft.

As is well known, this county is the home of the famous Sergeant Alvin C. York, whose wonderful exploit in the World War is familiar to everybody. History will record him as Fentress County's most illustrious citizen of all times.

Statistics of Fentress County: Population, 1920, 10,435. Assessed valuation of taxable property, 1921, $3,639,378. Area, 510 square miles. Number of farms, 1,214. Railway mileage, 25. Drained by Obed, Clear Fork, and Wolf Rivers, tributaries of the Cumberland River, and by Clear Creek, a tributary of

---
*The plan for this courthouse was made by Mark Twain's father, who was the first circuit court clerk of Fentress County and by far the largest land owner. It is said that he was the Si Hawkins of the "Gilded Age."

the Tennessee River. The eastern three-fourths of the county is high tableland. The northern portion is the Wolf River Valley, a fertile farming section, where is situated the farm given to Sergeant Alvin C. York, World War hero. Coal mines are operated in the western and eastern parts of the county and there are large areas of undeveloped coal lands. Plateau and the mountain sides are covered with fine timber. Natural grasses make fine grazing for cattle. Jamestown, the county seat, has a population of about 700, is a growing town, with good schools and churches, manufacturing establishments, prosperous stores, bank, etc. Fentress County is the only county in Tennessee, thus far, to produce crude oil in paying quantities. Jamestown, the county seat, has been made historic as the Obedstown of Mark Twain's "Gilded Age." Mark Twain's father at one time lived in Fentress County, owning large areas of land. The first American soldier wounded in France was from Fentress County, as was the World War's greatest hero. Scholastic population of county, 3,612; high schools, 8; elementary schools, 56.

FRANKLIN COUNTY

FRANKLIN COUNTY was erected on December 3, 1807, from Warren and Bedford Counties and was named in honor of Benjamin Franklin. The county seat was named Winchester for Gen. James Winchester. The site of Winchester was purchased from Christopher for one dollar. No courts, however, were held in Winchester until 1814. The first county court was held at the home of Maj. William Russell in 1808.

According to tradition the earliest settlers were: Maj. William Russell and Jesse Bean, both of whom arrived about 1800.

A large number of men eminent in the history of the state have been citizens of Franklin County. Among them may be mentioned: Judge Nathan Green, Thomas Fletcher, Edward Venable, Hopkins L. Turney and his son, Gov. Peter Turney, Dr. F. J. Campbell, A. S. Colyar, Gov. A. S. Marks, Thomas Gregory, and Gov. Isham G. Harris. The most famous educational institution of learning in the county and one of the most famous in the United States is the University of the South, founded in 1857 by Bishop Leonidas Polk at Sewanee. Besides this, however, two other notable institutions were established in this county—the Winchester Normal, founded in 1878, and the Mary Sharpe College, founded in 1850.

Statistics of Franklin County: population, 1920, 20,641.

Assessed valuation of taxable property, 1921, $14,207,894. Area, 570 square miles. Number of farms, 2,230. Railway mileage, 63. This county is drained by the Elk River and numerous small streams. Surface is hilly or table lands with a fine growth of timber. Staple products are corn, wheat, tobacco, cotton, hay and live stock. The N. C. & St. L. Railway intersects the county. Winchester, the county seat with a population of 2,203, is on a branch of the N. C. & St. L. Railway, 85 miles from Nashville, and has good schools and churches, a weekly newspaper, banks, manufacturing establishments, and flourishing stores. Decherd, with a population of 815, is another flourishing town with good schools and churches and prosperous business establishments. Scholastic population of county, 7,691; high schools, 3; elementary schools, 74.

GILES COUNTY

GILES COUNTY was erected on November 14, 1809, formed from a part of Maury County and named in honor of Gov. William B. Giles,* of Virginia, at the suggestion of Andrew Jackson. For the county seat a site was selected as near the center of the county as practicable and it was named Pulaski, in honor of Count Pulaski, of Poland, who has espoused the American cause in the Revolutionary War and was killed at Savannah in 1779.

The act establishing this county appointed James Ross, Nathaniel Moody, Tyree Rhodes, Gabriel Bumpass, and Thomas Whitson commissioners to select the county site and sell lots, reserving two acres for the public square on which the courthouse and stocks should be erected. The site selected was on the land "South and West of the Congressional Reservation Line"; and, consequently, being Indian land, the title to it could not be given until the restriction was removed on November 14, 1812.

The act establishing the county provided also for organizing a circuit court to be held on the second Monday in June and December, and also a court of Pleas and Quarter Session, whose first session was held on the third Monday in February at the home of Lewis Kirk, when the following-named officers qualified: German Lester, clerk; James Buford, sheriff; James Westmoreland, register; and Nelson Patterson, chairman.

*He was a Senator in Congress at the time Tennessee sought admittance into the Union and was an earnest and influential advocate of her admission when strong opposition developed.

The first circuit court was held probably in June, 1810. Thomas H. Stewart was judge; James Barry, clerk; and Amos Balch, attorney-general.

William Crawson and others made the first permanent settlement probably in 1805, near the mouth of Richland Creek. Some pioneers who settled on the lands south and west of the Reservation Line were repeatedly ejected by the United States soldiers stationed at Fort Hampton on Elk River, who destroyed their houses, crops and fences.

The first water power mill was established by Nathaniel Moody in 1809, on Robertson Creek. In 1810, Lewis Brown built the first horse-power mill. Daniel Allen built a power plant a little later, the saltpeter being obtained from a cave in Maury County. Lester Morris had the first cotton gin in 1810.

Early lawyers were: John Minns, W. H. Field, W. C. Flournoy, John H. Rivers, Gov. Aaron V. Brown, Adam Huntsman, Gov. Neill S. Brown, Robert Rose, Alfred Harris, Lunsford M. Bramlett, and Davidson Netherland.

Educational institutions of importance: Pulaski Academy, chartered November 30, 1809, Martin College, and Massey School.

Probably the first church established was by the Baptists in 1808, followed in 1809 by the Methodists and in 1810 by the Presbyterians.

It was in Giles County that Sam Davis was captured on November 20, 1863, and he was executed at Pulaski.

At Pulaski the Ku Klux Klan was organized by John C. Lester, James R. Crowe, John Kennedy, Calvin Jones, Richard R. Reed, and Frank O. McCord.

Statistics of Giles County: population, 1920, 30,948. Assessed valuation of taxable property, 1921, $21,651,634. Area, 656 square miles. Number of farms, 5,299. Railway mileage, 53. Drained by Elk River and Richland Creek. This county borders on Alabama, and its surface is undulating, with some sections well timbered. The soil is very productive, and it is one of the few cotton producing counties is Tennessee. Corn, cotton, fruit, and live stock are staple products. County is intersected by the L. & N. Railroad. Pulaski, the county seat, has a population of 2,780 and is on the L. & N. Railroad, 81 miles from Nashville. It is a flourishing town with two weekly newspapers, strong banks, fine churches and schools, and flourishing manufacturing and business establishments. Pulaski ships 8,000 to 10,000 bales of cotton annually. Lynville, with a population of 552, is another flourishing town. Scholastic population of county, 10,264; high schools, 11; elementary schools, 106.

GRUNDY COUNTY

GRUNDY COUNTY was erected on January 29, 1844, from parts of Coffee and Warren Counties and named for Felix Grundy, who, together with Samuel B. Barrett and others, had been dealing extensively in the mountain lands of that section. The act which created this county appointed Adrain Northcutt and William Dugan, residents of that part of the county taken from Warren, and John Burrows and Alfred Braley, residents of that part taken from Coffee, commissioners to organize Grundy County. The act also designated Beersheba Springs as a place for holding the first courts.

The first county court organized on August 6, 1844, with the following-named magistrates in attendance: Adrain Northcutt, John Fults, William Dugan, Ambrose Killian, Robert Tate, Isaac Campbell, Stephen M. Griswold, James Lockhart, John Burrows, Thomas Warren, and Daniel Sain.

The following officers, who had been elected on July 8, 1844, qualified: Philip Roberts, sheriff; Reuben Webb, county court clerk; Abraham Jones, register; John Burrows, trustee. The court then elected Stephen M. Griswold, entry-taker; William S. Mooney, surveyor; and Richard M. Stepp, coroner.

Beginning with the next session the courts were held continuously at the house of Jesse Wooten until October, 1848, when the county seat was established at Altamont. Later, Tracy City was made the county seat.

Tracy City was the first home of the great Tennessee Coal, Iron & Railway Company, now located near Birmingham. It was established by the late A. S. Colyar.

A large colony of Swiss located near Altamont has done much for the material progress of the county.

Statistics of Grundy County: population, 1920, 9,753. Assessed valuation of taxable property, 1921, $2,691,248. Area, 325 square miles. Number of farms, 563. Railway mileage, 30. Drained by numerous small streams. The surface is from 1,800 to 2,200 feet above sea level. The county is well adapted to the live-stock industry, having fine grazing lands. Staple products are corn, hay, fruits, and live stock. Tracy City, the principal town, has a population of 2,669, and is the center of large coal and iron industries. Large deposits of these minerals are found. Tracy City has good schools and churches, furnace, manufacturing establishments, and stores. It is on a branch of the N. C. & St. L. Railway. Altamont, the county seat, has a population of 114 and is a flourishing town. Scholastic population of county, 3,590, high schools, 4; elementary schools, 31.

HICKMAN COUNTY*

HICKMAN COUNTY was erected on December 3, 1807, from a part of Dickson County and was named in honor of Edmund Hickman, a surveyor, who, in 1785, together with James Robertson and Robert Weakley, came to survey entered lands on Pine River. On that trip Hickman was killed by the Indians near the mouth of Defeated Creek on Duck River, within a mile of the present city of Centerville, the county seat.

The first permanent settlement was made by Adam Wilson on Pine River in 1817. In 1819 the county was organized. The commissioners appointed to run and mark the lines of the county were: David Love, Joel Walker, John S. Primm, and Joseph Lynn.

The first county seat was Vernon (chosen in 1810), which was succeeded by Centerville, located in 1822, on land donated by John C. McLemore and Charles Stewart. The act which created the county provided that a court of Pleas and Quarter Sessions should meet on the first Monday of January, April, July, and October at the house of William Joslin on Pine River. The first justices of the peace were: Thomas Petty, William Wilson, James Miller, Robert Dunning, and Alexander Gray. William Wilson was chairman of the first session of the court. He was the father of the first white child (James Wilson, born on December 27, 1806) born in Hickman County. This court elected the following officers: William Phillips, sheriff; John Easley, trustee; Bartholomew G. Stewart, register; Joseph Lynn, ranger; and William Stone, clerk.

Statistics of Hickman County: population, 1920, 16,216. Assessed valuation of taxable property, 1921, $7,718,790. Area, 640 square miles. Number of farms, 1,928. Railway mileage, 46. Drained by Duck River. Soil fertile and well adapted to the live-stock industry. Staple products are wheat, corn, oats, grasses, and tobacco. Phosphate deposits are found in the county, and there are fine beds of iron ore. Centerville, the county seat, has a population of 882, with good schools, churches, weekly newspaper, bank, wagon factory, saw mill,

*The facts in this sketch were obtained largely from Spence's History of Hickman County.

and prosperous mercantile establishments. Scholastic population of county, 5,253; high schools, 6; elementary schools, 93.

HOUSTON COUNTY

HOUSTON COUNTY was erected on January 21, 1871, from parts of Dickson, Humphreys, and Stewart Counties and was named in honor of Sam Houston. The act provided for a part of Montgomery County to be included, also subject to the vote of the people of the part in question. But these people voted against inclusion in the new county.

The first county court was held in the Union Church, in Erin, on April 3, 1871. N. McKinnon was the chairman. On April 21, 1871, Arlington was selected as the county seat, and the courthouse was completed about a year later, and the county court convened in it on May 6, 1872. In 1878, Erin became the county seat.

The first officers of the county were: J. S. Lee, clerk; J. J. Pollard, court clerk, R. C. Cushing, sheriff; J. W. Hall, trustee; S. T. Allen, trustee; C. S. Humphreys, register.

The first circuit court met on April 4, 1871.

The early settlements began about 1798 or 1799 when Henry Edwards and his family located at Stewart Station. Other pioneers followed in the next few years. One of them was the father of Judge Jo C. Guild, who speaks interestingly and affectionately of the people of Houston County in his book "Old Times in Tennessee." Other pioneers were Fred Boone, a relative of Daniel Boone, Daniel Buchanan, a man of tremendous strength, and Dr. Marable. It is said that William Murrell, a brother of John A. Murrell, taught school in what is now Houston County between 1820 and 1830.

Statistics of Houston County: population, 1920, 6,212. Assessed valuation of taxable property, 1921, $3,111,066. Area, 210 square miles. Number of farms, 724. Railway mileage, 20. Drained by the Cumberland and Tennessee Rivers. Surface is hilly and soil fertile. Some sections are well covered with timber. Staple products are corn, tobacco, grass, and fruits. Erin, the county seat, with a population of 855, is near the Cumberland River, 28 miles from Clarksville. It has good churches and schools, a weekly newspaper, bank, and manufacturing establishments. Scholastic population of county, 2,454; high schools, 1; elementary schools, 30.

HUMPHREYS COUNTY

HUMPHREYS COUNTY was erected on October 19, 1809, out of part of Stewart County and was named in honor of Perry W. Humphreys, a judge of the Superior Court of Law and Equity, 1807-1809, and held the first court in this county.

The act creating the county provided that the first court should be held at the house of Samuel Parker, Jr., on Trace Creek, about two miles from Waverly.

The first county seat was established in 1816 at Reynoldsville, which was named for John B. Reynolds, then a representative in Congress. The Supreme Court, also, at that time held its sessions in Reynoldsville for that division of the state. The site of the county seat was on fifty acres of land donated by Alexander Brevard. When Benton County was erected in 1835, largely from territory previously included in Humphreys County, the county seat was moved to Waverly, which was named for Scott's Waverly novels. The site of Waverly was donated by Davis Childress and the survey was made by Isaac Little in 1836.

Probably the first settlement in the county was made by Moses Box in 1800 at a point on Trace Creek, but development was slow on account of the depredations of the Indians.

Humphreys County has been conspicious in all of the wars in which Tennessee has taken part, and in the War between the States furnished more soldiers than it had voters. It was at Johnsonville in this county where Forrest captured the Federal gunboats and destroyed five million dollars worth of Federal property.

Statistics of Humphreys County: population, 1920, 13,482. Assessed valuation of taxable property, 1921, $7,514,498. Area, 420 square miles. Number of farms, 1,805. Railway mileage, 27. Drained by the Tennessee and Duck Rivers. Fine timber in some sections. Its surface is partly hilly, but the land along the rivers is very fertile. This is the largest peanut producing county in the state, and this is an important industry. Other staples are wheat, corn, cotton, grasses, and live stock. The Nashville, Chattanooga & St. Louis Railway traverses the county. Waverly, the county seat, has a population of 1,054, with good churches, schools, weekly newspaper, general stores, and manufacturing establishments. McEwen is another flourishing town in Humphreys County and has a population of 635, with good schools, churches, bank, newspaper, and business houses. Scholastic population of county, 4,817; high schools, 4; elementary schools, 71.

JACKSON COUNTY

JACKSON COUNTY was erected in 1801 from a part of Smith County and was named in honor of Andrew Jackson, who, at that time, was a judge of the Superior Court of Law and Equity, having, since 1796, resigned both as a member of the House of Representatives and as a member of the Senate of the United States.

Early settlers came in soon after the establishment of Nashville; and as the Indians were a menace a fort, named Fort Blount after Gov. William Blount, was erected in this county on the Cumberland River as a protection for the settlers and travelers.

Gainesboro, the county seat of Jackson County, named for Gen. Edmund Pendleton Gaines, was established in 1817 and incorporated in 1820.

Statistics of Jackson County: population, 1920, 14,955. Assessed valuation of taxable property, 1921, $5,981,662. Area, 280 square miles. Number of farms, 2,403. Railway mileage, none. Drained by Cumberland River and tributaries. Surface is hilly and well covered with timber. Soil along the river and in the valleys is very fertile. Staple products are corn, wheat, tobacco, grass, and live stock. Splendid county for fruit-growing. Gainesboro, the county seat, has a population of 351 and is near the Cumberland River. It has good schools and churches, one bank, a weekly newspaper, and flourishing stores. Granville is another flourishing town in the county. Scholastic population of county, 6,022; high schools, 4; elementary schools, 60.

LAWRENCE COUNTY

LAWRENCE COUNTY was erected in 1817 out of part of Hickman and part of Maury Counties and named in honor of Capt. James Lawrence, of the Chesapeake, who when mortally wounded said to his men: "Don't give up the ship."

The earliest settlement was made near Henryville on the Big Buffalo River and soon were established (about 1815) a grain mill, a distillery and a Primitive Baptist Church. From this time population increased rapidly, and in a few years Lawrence became one of the most enterprising of the pioneer counties of the section. Prominent among the early settlers were: the Parkes family, the Striblings, Sykes brothers, Simms, and Bentleys.

Soon after the county was organized David Crockett arrived and lived there for several years. He became a member of the county court and of the building committee which erected the first courthouse. Having gotten in debt, he sold his lands and moved to West Tennessee. Last year a splendid monument was erected to his memory in Lawrenceburg.

Lawrenceburg was chartered on November 23, 1819. In the years preceding the Civil War, Wayland Springs was noted as a resort for health and pleasure.

Lawrence County is justly proud of its record in war. On the public square of Lawrenceburg stands a monument to those who lost their lives in the Mexican War, the only memorial of the kind, it is believed, in the State of Tennessee. It was erected in 1849, and the state contributed $1,500 toward the cost of it.

Statistics of Lawrence County: population, 1920, 23,593. Assessed valuation of taxable property, 1921, $11,386,098. Area, 676 square miles. Number of farms, 3,590. Railway mileage, 62. Drained by tributaries of the Tennessee River. Surface diversified and well timbered. Good deposits of iron ore and phosphate are found in the county. Staple products are corn, wheat, cotton, oats, grass, and live stock. Lawrenceburg, the county seat, has a population of 2,461 and is a flourishing town, with good schools and churches, two weekly newspapers, banks, manufacturing establishments, general stores, and electric light plant. Scholastic population of county, 8,375; high school, 1; elementary schools, 60.

LEWIS COUNTY

LEWIS COUNTY was created on December 23, 1843, from parts of Hickman, Maury, Lawrence, and Wayne Counties and named in honor of Meriwether Lewis,* who with William Clark conducted the famous Lewis and Clark expedition to Oregon in 1803-1806.

A Mr. Dobbins and Robert Grinder, who established a tavern, were among the first settlers, about 1807.

The first county seat was Newburg, which was supplanted by Hohenwald after the latter place had become prominent on account of the work and enterprise of a colony of Swiss who

---

*On October 11, 1809, he either committed suicide or was murdered at Grinder's Tavern on the Natchez Trace, about eight miles from Hohenwald, while he was on his way to Washington from St. Louis in Louisiana Territory of which he had been appointed governor. In 1848, the State of Tennessee erected a monument to his memory on the spot where he was buried. This monument, about twenty-five feet high, in an obscure place, is now neglected, in a bad condition, and forgotten by almost everybody.

located there. Hohenwald was named by these colonists and means high forest.

Lewis County is not blessed agriculturally as most of the counties of Tennessee, but it has valuable deposits of phosphate and iron which are adding materially to its wealth.

Statistics of Lewis County: population, 1920, 5,707. Assessed valuation of taxable property, 1921, $3,147,871. Area, 280 square miles. Number of farms, 537. Railway mileage, 34. Drained by several small streams, tributaries to Duck River. Intersected by a branch of the N. C. & St. L. Railway. Staple products are peanuts, corn, wheat, oats, grass, and live stock. Iron ore, oxide of iron, and ochre are found in the county. Hohenwald, the county seat, has a population of 742, a weekly newspaper, two banks, fine schools and churches, and flourishing business houses. Scholastic population of county, 2,089; high schools, 1; elementary schools, 36.

LINCOLN COUNTY

LINCOLN COUNTY was erected on November 14, 1809, from a part of Bedford County and was named for Gen. Benjamin Lincoln, who performed great services in the Revolutionary War.

By the act which created this county, John Whitaker, Sr., Wright Williams, Eli Garrett, Littleton Duty, and Jeffe Woodruff were appointed commissioners to secure one hundred acres of land near the center of the county for a county seat to be named Fayetteville. They bought the land for $700 from Ezekiel Norris, who in 1806 had settled on Norris Creek on his grant of 1,280 acres.

The act also provided that the sessions of the Court of Pleas and Quarter Sessions should be held at the house of Brice M. Garner until a place should be provided in Fayetteville. The first session was held on February 26, 1810. The magistrates were qualified by Oliver Williams, and Thomas H. Benton acted as clerk pro tem. Both of these men were from Williamson County. At this session Brice M. Garner was elected county court clerk. Thomas Stewart was elected judge of the circuit court and James Bright, clerk.

Notable men of the early days were: Archibald Yell and Joseph Greer, the latter of whom, a giant in stature, carried to Congress at Philadelphia the news of the battle of King's Mountain.

Statistics of Lincoln County: population, 1920, 25,786. Assessed valuation of taxable property, 1921, $18,596,485. Area,

540 square miles. Number of farms, 4,367. Railway mileage, 62. Drained by Elk River. Soil is very fertile in a large portion of the county. Leading crops are corn, wheat, and grass. The live-stock industry is flourishing in this county. Fayetteville, the county seat, has a population of 3,629 and is one of the best towns in this section of the state. It has electric light and water systems, two weekly newspapers, four banks, fine schools and churches, and several manufacturing establishments. Petersburg, Flintville, Elora, and Mulberry are other towns in the county. Scholastic population of the county, 8,021; high schools, 22; elementary schools, 55.

MACON COUNTY

MACON COUNTY was erected on January 18, 1842, from parts of Smith and Sumner Counties and was named for Nathaniel Macon, of whom Thomas H. Benton said: "He spoke more good sense while getting in his chair and getting out of it than many delivered in long and elaborate speeches."

The first county court appointed Britton Holland, William Dunn, Samuel Sullivan, Eason Howell, and Jefferson Short as commissioners to hold an election to select a county seat. The place selected was on land of John B. Johnson on the dividing ridge between the Cumberland and Big Barren Rivers and was named LaFayette in honor of the Marquis de LaFayette.

The first county court met at the house of William Dunn, and Patrick Ferguson was chairman of it. The first county officers were: King Kerley, sheriff; William Weaver, register; Daniel O. Pursley, trustee; William Blackmore, county surveyor; David Claiborne, coroner.

The first constables were: Thomas A. Meador, George White, Edward Barbee, Ensley Wilmore, B. Y. Turnor, Bennett Wright, and James G. Stone.

The first justices of the peace were: Anderson Bratton, William Robertson, Charles Simmons, Haylum Pursley, Taylor O. Gillum, Jefferson B. Short, Ichabod Young, Jacob J. Johnson, Lewis Meador, William Roark, James J. York, James Patterson, and James Henderson.

The first courthouse was built in 1844. The first circuit court was held in May, 1842 at the house of William Dunn and was presided over by Judge Abraham Caruthers.

Statistics of Macon County: population, 1920, 14,922. Assessed valuation of taxable property, 1921, $4,308,877. Area, 450 square miles. Number of farms, 2,743. Railway mileage, none. Drained by tributaries of Cumberland and Big Barren Rivers. Its surface is generally uneven and well timbered. Staple products are corn, wheat, tobacco, grass, and live stock. Good gardening and truck-growing section. LaFayette, the county seat, has a population of 547, good schools and churches, flourishing business establishments, a weekly newspaper, and one bank. Red Boiling Springs, a noted health resort, is in this county. Scholastic population, 5,128; high schools, 2; elementary schools, 59.

MARSHALL COUNTY

MARSHALL COUNTY was erected February 26, 1836, from parts of Lincoln, Bedford, and Maury Counties, to which was added a part of Giles in 1870. It was named in honor of John Marshall, chief justice.

The first county court was organized on October 3, 1836, at the house of Abner Houston with the following justices of the peace in attendance: William McClure, Thomas Ross, William Wilkes, Peter Williams, Thomas Wilson, David McGahey, James Adams, George Cunningham, James V. Ewing, John Fields, Adam Miller, Joseph Cleek, Ephriam Hunter, Asa Holland, James Patterson, Jason Sheffield, Sherwood Dunnigan, and Andrew Laird. The following officers were elected: John R. Hill, sheriff; Martin W. Oakley, county court clerk; John W. Record, trustee; John Elliott, register; Joseph McCorf, coroner; Isaac H. Williams, ranger; Hugh McClelland, surveyor.

By the act which created the county, Richard Warner, William Smith, Holman R. Fowler, George W. McBride, and William D. Orr were appointed commissioners to select the county seat to be named Lewisburg, in honor of Meriwether Lewis. Abner Houston gave fifty acres for the county site. Lewisburg was incorporated on December 16, 1837.

Early settlers were: Asa Fonville, in 1807; James Patterson, in 1808; William McClure, in 1809; the Becks, Wallaces, and Allens. Gen. Nathan Bedford Forrest, who was born near Chapel Hill, was a descendent of the Becks. Capt. Andrew Patterson, who commanded a company at the battle of New Orleans, made a settlement near Chapel Hill about 1800.

The first circuit court was held at Abner Houston's house in November, 1836, Judge Edmund Dillahunty presiding.

The first chancery court was established in 1836, Lunsford M. Bramlett, chancellor.

The first postmaster was John Hatchett. The first paper published was the Marshall Democrat in 1847. The second was the Lewisburg Gazette in 1848.

The first church was Bethbersi, organized June 1, 1810, by Rev. Samuel Findley, Presbyterian. The first minister was Rev. John Gillespie.

Statistics of Marshall County: population, 1920, 17,375. Assessed valuation of taxable property, 1921, $13,927,210. Area, 377 square miles. Number of farms, 2,560. Railway mileage, 60. Drained by Duck River. Northern part of the county is generally level; southern portion is hilly with valleys that are fertile. Staple products are corn, oats, wheat, fruit, and live stock. A branch of the Nashville, Chattanooga & St. Louis Railway passes through the county, and it is also intersected by the Lewisburg & Northern, a branch of the Louisville & Nashville. Lewisburg, the county seat, has a population of 2,711, fine schools and churches, two weekly newspapers, two banks, and flourishing manufacturing and commercial establishments. Chapel Hill, Farmington, and Cornersville are other towns. Scholastic population, 5,671; high schools, 9; elementary schools, 45.

MAURY COUNTY

MAURY COUNTY was erected November 24, 1807, from a part of Williamson County and was named in honor of Major Abram P. Maury. It is one of the best counties in the state. From an agricultural point of view no county in the state is superior to it.

The first county court was held at the house of Col. Joseph Brown, about three miles south of Columbia. He was licensed to keep an "ordinary" and gave bond to furnish "good, wholesome, and clean lodging and diet for travelers, stabling with hay, oats, corn, fodder, and pasturage, as the season of the year may require, and not to suffer or permit gambling, nor on the Sabbath day permit any person to tipple or drink more than necessary."

The magistrates of this first court were: John Dickey, John Miller, William Gilchrist, William Frierson, Isaac Roberts, John Spencer, John Lindsey, Joshua Williams, James Love, Lemuel Pruett, and William Dooley. Peter R. Booker was appointed solicitor. Joseph Herndon was the first resident attorney admitted to practice.

The commissioners appointed by the Legislature in 1808 to select the county seat were: Joshua Williams, William Frierson, Isaac Roberts, John Lindsey, and Joseph Brown. They selected Columbia, which was incorporated in 1817. The first physicians were: Drs. O'Reilly and Estes. Later physicians were: Drs. DePriest, McNeil, Sansom, McJimsey, and Graves.

The first paper, The Western Chronicle, was founded in 1811 by James Walker, who married a sister of President Polk in 1813.

The early settlers in Maury County came from North Carolina and Virginia. Attention to this county was brought early and particularly because of the location there of the 25,000 acres given Gen. Nathaniel Greene because of his services in the Revolutionary War.

One of the earliest colonies, however, came from South Carolina in 1807 and in 1808, led by John Dickey and settled in the Zion Church neighborhood. Besides Dickey, prominent settlers were: Moses Frierson, James Blakeley, William Frierson, Eli Frierson, James Armstrong, Thomas Stephenson, Nathaniel Stephenson, "Old Davy" Matthews, Samuel Witherspoon, John Stephenson, James Frierson, P. Fulton, Alexander Dobbins, Moses Freeman, the Flemings and Mayes. They built a church, which served also as a schoolhouse in which the minister, Rev. Henderson, was a teacher. At one time James K. Polk was one of his pupils.

Not far from Mt. Zion was the Polk settlement. From the first settlers, in 1807, William Dever and his sister, William Polk bought their 5,000-acre grant. He divided the estate among his four sons: Bishop Leonidas Polk, Lucius P. Polk, George N. Polk, and Rufus K. Polk. This became known as the "Polk Neighborhood." Near it was the home of Gen. Gideon J. Pillow.

Another prominent settlement was the Spring Hill community which was started about 1808-1810 by Abraham Hammond, Colonel Russell, Nathaniel Cheairs, James Black and others. James Black was the grandfather of Col. Henry Watterson and father-in-law of Judge Stanley Matthews of the United States Supreme Court.

Few counties have been so prolific in prominent, noted, and great men. Among them were: President James K. Polk, Gen. Felix K. Zollicoffer, Gen. Ewell Stanley Matthews, Matthew Fontaine Maury, Henry F. Cooper, A. P. Nicholson, William Fields,* Bishop Leonidas Polk, Bishop Otey, Gideon J. Pillow, Terry H. Cahal, William Polk, Thomas Wrenne, Maj.

*The compiler of the famous Scrapbook.

James Holland, Dr. Samuel Mayes, James Armstrong, a member of Lee's Legion, David Matthews, who served under Gen. Francis Marion, Gen. Richard Winn, Edward Ward Carmack, and many others.

Statistics of Maury County: population, 1920, 35,403. Assessed valuation of taxable property, 1921, $29,694,070. Area, 596 square miles. Number of farms, 3,728. Railway mileage, 102. Drained by Duck River. Land is very fertile and is one of the richest agricultural counties in the state. Staple products are corn, wheat, oats, hay, fruits, and live stock. The dairying industry is extensive, the county having some of the finest herds in the state. There are immense phosphate deposits in the county which have been worked for years. Columbia, the county seat, has a population of 5,526, is on the Duck River, and has two railroads. It is the seat of Columbia Institute for Girls and Columbia Military Academy and has a fine system of public schools, splendid churches, daily and weekly newspapers, four banks, several manufacturing establishments, mills, etc. It is one of the largest mule markets in the country. Mount Pleasant, the center of the phosphate mining industry, has a population of 2,093 and has good schools and churches, two banks, a weekly newspaper, cotton mill, two creameries and prosperous manufacturing and mercantile establishments. Other prosperous towns are Culleoka and Spring Hill. The latter place has excellent private schools. Scholastic population of county, 11,352; high schools, 13, elementary schools, 100.

MONTGOMERY COUNTY

MONTGOMERY COUNTY was named for John Montgomery, erected in 1796, when Tennessee county gave up its name to the state and its territory was divided into Montgomery and Robertson County. Its first permanent settlement was made by Moses Renfroe and his company when they left Col. John Donelson's colony on April 12, 1780, as they were on their way up the Cumberland to the great French Lick (Nashville). Renfroe ascended the Red River to the mouth of Carson's Creek where he built Renfroe's Station (sometimes called Red River Station). Among these settlers were: Moses, Isaac, Joseph, and James Renfroe, Nathan and Solomon Turpin, Isaac Mayfield, James Hollis, James Johns, and a widow named Jones.

On account of the fear of an Indian attack they left the station for the Bluff (Nashville), and at Battle Creek were attacked and twenty persons killed. The earliest stations in this county were Prince's, Clarksville, and Nevill's. Francis Prince and James Ford were the leaders at Prince's. Col. James Ford was probably the most striking figure in the county at that period. John Montgomery and Martin Armstrong laid off the land and made the plan of a town on the north bank of the Cumberland just above the mouth of Red River and entered the land in 1784. They named the town Clarksville, in honor of George Rogers Clark. In 1785 the Legislature of North Carolina established the town of Clarksville and named in the act the following commissioners: John Montgomery, Anthony Crutcher, William Polk, Anthony Bledsoe, and Lardner Clark. This was the second town established in Middle Tennessee.

In 1788 a tobacco inspection was established at Clarksville, the first in the state. In the same year Tennessee County was erected out of which Montgomery County was established, and a Court of Pleas and Quarter Sessions was held at the house of Isaac Titsworth, on Person's Creek for the first and second sessions. For the third session it met at the house of William Grimbs; and all subsequent sessions were held at Clarksville, where, on the public square, a rude, log courthouse was built.

The earliest inhabitants of Clarksville were: John Montgomery, Anthony and William Crutcher, Amos Bird, George Bell, Robert Nelson, and Aeneas McAllister. In 1794-1795 there were: John Easton, Daniel James, James Adams, William Montgomery, Philip Gilbert, Robert Dunnung, Hugh McCallum, Benjamin Hawkins, and Andrew Snoddy.

Soon after Clarksville was established George and Joseph B. Medill, from South Carolina, built a fort on Red River between Prince's and Clarksville.

The first and most important settlement on the south side of the Cumberland was Palmyra at the mouth of Deason's Creek. It was the first port of entry in the West, a fact which indicates its importance at that time. It was laid out by Dr. Morgan Brown, father of the eminent jurist, Judge William L. Brown, and was chartered in 1796. From 1780 to 1795, the people suffered much from the Indians who were instigated by the Spanish. Prominent among their deeds of horrors were the Titsworth Massacre in 1794; the murder of John Dier and Benjamin Lindsey, in 1793; the heroic death of John Montgomery, in 1794; the murder of Maj. Evan Shelby, brother of

Isaac Shelby, in 1793; the ambushing and killing of three sons of Col. Valentine Sevier, brother of John Sevier, and of their two companions in 1792; and the sanguinary attack on Colonel Sevier's Station, in 1794.

Most of the early inhabitants of Montgomery County came from North Carolina, South Carolina, Virginia, and Pennsylvania. Among those from North Carolina were: Haydon Wells, James, Charles, and Duncan Stewart, Anthony and William Crutcher, and Robert Nelson. Among those from South Carolina were: James Ford, Francis, William, and Robert Prince, George Bell, George Nevill, Joseph B. Nevill, and Dr. Morgan Brown. From Virginia, via Watauga, were: Evan and Moses Shelby, Valentine Sevier, John Montgomery, and John H. Poston. From Pennsylvania were: James Elder and Aeneas McAllister.

Schools began in the county immediately after the Indian atrocities ended. Mrs. Gibbs and Mrs. Hise opened a school for young ladies at Clarksville in the thirties. In 1837 the Female Academy was opened. There was also a Male Academy. The greatest institution of all, however, was the Southwestern Presbyterian University.

Clarksville, also, has been the home of many literary lights, among them being Father Ryan, William A. Peffer (later a United States Senator from Kansas), Martha McCulloch Williams, Elizabeth N. Gilmer ("Dorothy Dix"), Judge C. W. Tyler, and Prof. G. F. Nicholassen.

Statistics of Montgomery County: population, 1920, 32,265. Assessed valuation of taxable property, 1921, $19,207,350. Area, 540 square miles. Number of farms, 4,121. Railway mileage, 83. County borders on Kentucky and is intersected by the Cumberland River. Its surface is undulating and partly timbered. Its soil is fertile and it is one of the best tobacco-producing counties in the state. Fine limestone and iron ore deposits are found in the county. Staple products are tobacco, corn, wheat, oats, and live stock. The county is traversed by the L. & N. and the Tennessee Central Railroads. Clarksville, the county seat, has a population of 8,110. It is on two railroads and the Cumberland River. It is an up-to-date city with all conveniences, a large tobacco market, has fine schools and churches, daily and weekly newspapers, several manufacturing establishments, and is a jobbing center for a large territory. New Providence, St. Bethlehem, Palmyra, and Corbandale are other towns in the county. Scholastic population in the county, 10,332; high schools, 6; elementary schools, 96.

MOORE COUNTY

MOORE COUNTY was erected on December 14, 1871, out of portions of Lincoln, Franklin, Coffee, and Bedford Counties, to be called Moore County, in honor of the late Gen. William Moore, who was one of the early settlers of Lincoln County, a soldier of the War of 1812 and a member for several terms of the General Assembly.

This county was established in violation of a provision of the constitution which requires that each county shall have not less than 275 square miles. The reason was that one of its lines was laid out less than 11 miles from the courthouse of Lincoln County, which promptly demanded enough of the territory of the new county to place the boundary line at the proper distance thus reducing the area of Moore County to 160 square miles.

The first settlements were made about 1800 by pioneers from North Carolina and Georgia, attracted by the game, once lived here on the head waters of East Mulberry Creek. Thomas Roundtree, one of the first settlers, owned the land on which Lynchburg is situated. He laid off the town about 1820, and it was incorporated in 1841.

Moses Crawford, one of the first settlers, is authority for the statement that there was in the early days a den of thieves near Lynchburg and that "stealing was as common as going to church." It became necessary, therefore, to have a vigilance committee to maintain law and order. Offences were punished at the whipping post. A small, weakly man named Lynch, who was living there, was so frequently chosen to wield the lash that in time the place was called Lynchburg, so tradition says.

The first county court met at the house of Tolley and Eaton, in Lynchburg, in June, 1873, and in the same year Lynchburg was selected as the county seat.

In the early days camp meetings were held at the camp grounds. Enoch's camp ground, four miles northeast of Lynchburg, was a famous meeting place of the Methodists in those times.

Statistics of Moore County: population, 1920, 4,491. Assessed valuation of taxable property, 1921, $1,900,629. Area, 170 square miles. Number of farms, 846. Railway mileage, none. It is drained by Elk River, and its surface is hilly and partly covered with timber. The soil is fertile, and principal products are corn, wheat, oats, and live stock. Lynchburg, the county seat, has a population of 365, good schools and churches, a weekly newspaper, two banks, and flourishing business establishments. It is noted as a mule market. Scholastic population of county, 1,600; high schools, 1; elementary schools, 20.

OVERTON COUNTY

OVERTON COUNTY was erected in 1806 from a part of Jackson County and was named in honor of Judge John Overton, the most intimate friend of Andrew Jackson. The earliest settlers were Col. Stephen Copeland and his son, "Big Joe" Copeland. Other early settlers were: John Goodpasture, father of the distinguished jurist, Judge Jefferson D. Goodpasture; Capt. Jesse Arnold; Capt. Simeon Hinds, father of the learned chemist and teacher, Dr. J. I. D. Hinds, of Lebanon; Benjamin Totten, father of Judge A. W. O. Totten; Moses Fisk; Judge Alvin Cullom; Adam Huntsman; and some descendants of John Sevier.

The first court was held at a place called later Jones' Store, about five miles north of Livingston, and became a rival for the honor of being the county seat and a lively animosity arose between the two towns. Finally, in an election in 1833, Livingston was victorious by a small majority.

The oldest town in the county is Hilham, founded in 1805 by Moses Fisk. It was there that the Fisk Female Academy was located, the first school distinctly for girls chartered in the South and one of the first in the entire United States.

Statistics of Overton County: population, 1920, 17,617. Assessed valuation of taxable property, 1921, $4,471,888. Area, 376 square miles. Number of farms, 2,714. Railway mileage, 30. Drained by Obed and Roaring Rivers, tributaries of the Cumberland River. Its surface is hilly and its soil very fertile. Fine grazing lands for cattle and sheep. Staple products are corn, wheat, hay, and live stock. The county is well timbered and there are good deposits of coal. Livingston, the county seat, is the terminus of the Tennessee, Kentucky & Northern, a short line extending from the Tennessee Central, and has a population of 1,215. It has good schools and churches, two weekly newspapers, two banks, and several manufacturing establishments, and is a flourishing town. Scholastic population of county, 6,597; high schools, 6; elementary schools, 84.

PERRY COUNTY

PERRY COUNTY was erected on November 14, 1821, from a part of Hickman County and was named in honor of Commodore Oliver H. Perry. It embraced at first the territory now in Perry and Decatur Counties.

The first county court was organized on the first Monday in January, 1820, at the house of James Dickson, on Lick Creek, when Joseph Brown was chosen chairman and the following magistrates were qualified: James Dickson, Joseph Brown, William Holmes, William Britt, John L. Houston, Enoch Hooper, Oswald Griffin, a Mr. Nunn, and Green B. Newsom. The following officers were elected: William Harmon, clerk; Aaron Lewis, trustee; John A. Rains, register; Jacob Harmon, ranger; Mark Murphy, coroner; West Wood, sheriff.

The county seat was established in 1771, at Perryville, on the west side of the Tennessee River. This remained the county seat until 1846, when the Tennessee River was made the boundary line and the western part was erected into Decatur County.

In the early days Perryville was a political and business center of importance. David Crockett, Andrew Jackson, Sam Houston, James K. Polk, and other visited it.

For two years after the division the courts of Perry County were held at Harrisburg, now Bethel, three miles south of Linden, which was selected as a county seat in 1848 by a majority of six votes. In the same year the first courthouse was built of logs.

The first school in the county was on Tom's Creek, taught by Ferny Stanley in 1820. The first steamboat, the General Greene, arrived in 1819. The first merchant was John Yates, who had a store on Tom's Creek in 1819. John Tracy built the first water mill on Cedar Creek in 1820.

The first circuit court was held at James Dickson's on Lick Creek in 1820. Judge Humphreys presided.

The first church was built in 1821 on Lick Creek by the Primitive Baptists and the first ministers who held services were Rev. William Hodge and Rev. Samuel Akins.

Statistics of Perry County: population, 1920, 7,765. Assessed valuation of taxable property, 1921, $3,379,600. Area, 420, square miles. Number of farms, 1,235. Railway mileage, none. Drained by Tennessee River and its tributaries. Surface diversified by high ridges and rich valleys, and portions of it are well timbered. It is one of the principal peanut-producing counties of the state. Other staple products are corn, wheat, buck-wheat, and live stock. Linden, the county seat, has a population of about 500 and is a town of good schools and churches and flourishing business establishments. It is 13 miles from the Tennessee River and 80 miles from Nashville. Scholastic population of county, 2,546; high schools, 3; elementary schools, 48.

PICKETT COUNTY

PICKETT COUNTY was erected in 1879 from parts of Overton and Fentress Counties and was named for H. L. Pickett, a resident of Wilson County. Its early history is the history of the counties from which it was taken.

Statistics of Pickett County: population, 1920, 5,205. Assessed valuation of taxable property, 1921, $1,188,975. Area, 240 square miles. Number of farms, 935. Railway mileage, none. Its surface is hilly, and it is well watered by Obed and Wolf Rivers. Some sections are covered with fine timber. Staple products are corn, wheat, oats, grass, and live stock. Byrdstown, the county seat, has a population of 125 and has good schools and churches, a bank, and flourishing business houses. Scholastic population of county, 1,914; high schools, none, elementary schools, 30.

PUTNAM COUNTY

PUTNAM COUNTY was erected on February 1, 1842, from parts of White, Overton, Jackson, Smith, and DeKalb Counties and was named in honor of Gen. Israel Putnam of the Revolutionary War.

In accordance with the provisions of the act creating this county, the county and circuit courts were established and their officers were elected and functioned until 1844 when an injunction restraining the officers from performing their duties of their offices was applied for and was granted. February 11, 1854, however, Putnam County was re-established largely through the efforts of Major Cooke, after whom Cookeville, the county seat was named. He was one of the most prominent citizens of the county and, at the time, was an influential member of the State Senate. The way for the re-establishment of the county was facilitated by the decision of the State Supreme Court that after the organization of the county was complete and the original commissioners had performed their duty, it was not within the jurisdiction of the courts of justice to enjoin the civil officers from proceeding in their official duties.

The commissioners named in the reorganization act located the county seat and laid off the town which was named Cookeville. Monticello was a competitor for this honor. This commission was composed of Joshua R. Stone and Dr. Green H. Baker, of White County; Austin Morgan and Maj. John Brown, of Jackson County; William Davis and Isaiah Warthon, of Overton County; William B. Stokes and Bird S. Rhea, of DeKalb County; Benjamin A. Vaden and Nathan Ward, of Smith County.

Putnam County furnished many gallant officers in the War between the States. Among them were: Sidney S. Stanton, John B. Vance, Harvey H. Dillard, Holland Denton, Walton Smith, S. H. McDearmon, John H. Quarles, W. B. Carten, S. J. Johnson, Rison Robinson, C. J. Davis, S. G. Slaughter, William Ensor, Abraham Hord. Gen Alvin C. Gillem, one of the three general officers furnished the Union Army from Tennessee, was a Putnam Countian.

Monterey (called in the early days Standing Stone) and Bloomington Springs are noted summer resorts. There are important deposits of coal, phosphate, lithograph stone, sandstone, and petroleum.

Statistics of Putnam County: population, 1920, 22,231. Assessed valuation of taxable property, 1921, $9,784,713. Area, 430 square miles. Number of farms, 2,983. Railway mileage, 49. Drained by tributaries of the Caney Fork and the Cumberland Rivers. Its surface is undulating and partly covered with fine timber. County is well adapted to stock-raising and fruit-growing. Staple products are corn, grass, and live stock. Fine coal deposits are found in the mountain section of the county. The Tennessee Central Railway traverses the county. Cookeville, the county seat, has a population of 2,395 and has fine churches and schools. It is the seat of the Tennessee Polytechnic Institute. It has a fine electric light plant, water system, weekly newspaper, two banks, several manufacturing establishments, prosperous stores, and is the jobbing center for a considerable territory. Monterey, on top of a mountain, has a population of 1,445 and is the center of the spoke and handle and stave industry for that section. It has good schools and churches and prosperous business establishments. Algood and Baxter are other towns in the county. Scholastic population of county, 7,739; high schools, 5; elementary schools, 70.

ROBERTSON COUNTY

THE creation of Robertson County was synchronous with that of Montgomery County, both having been erected from Tennessee County on April 9, 1796. It was named in honor of James Robertson.

The first settler in this county was Thomas Kilgore. In 1776 or 1777 he lived for some time in a cave on the South Fork of Red River, near what is now the village of Cross Plains. After spending about a year there, he returned to his family in North Carolina and took part in the battle of King's Mountain. On his return he was accompanied by Moses Maulden, Ambrose Maulson, Samuel Mason, Josiah Hankins, and several others with their families. They arrived toward the latter part of 1780 and built a fort, called Kilgore's Fort or Kilgore's Station on Kilgore's land. After a few months, however, they abandoned the station because of the depredations of the Indians. Kilgore returned later and lived there until his death at the age of one hundred and eight.

From Tennessee County, of which Robertson was a part, the delegates to the Constitutional Convention of 1796 were: Thomas Johnson, James Ford, William Fort, William Prince, and Robert Prince. The original constitution is in the handwriting of William Fort, who was considered the best penman among the delegates.

On July 18, 1776, the first county court organized at the house of Jacob McCarty, with the following-named magistrates present: William Fort, chairman, Benjamin Menees, William Miles, Isaac Phillips, Bazil Boren, Martin Duncan, John Phillips, James Crabtree, and Zebulon Hart. Samuel Donelson was made county solicitor. The next term of the court was held at the house of Benjamin McIntosh, and this continued to be the place of the meeting until July, 1798, when it met at the store of George Bell, where Springfield now is. When the courthouse was built in 1799 the sessions were held there.

In April, 1796, thirty acres were donated to the county by Archer Cheatham for a county site. In 1798 twenty acres more were bought from Thomas Johnson, and Springfield became the county seat.

Early physicians were Drs. Levi Noyes, Clark B. Bell, and Archie Thomas.

The circuit court was organized on April 10, 1810. It was presided over by Judge Parry W. Humphreys. The first lawyer was Thornton A. Cook. Other early lawyers were: W. H. Dortch and W. W. Pepper.

According to tradition, William Black taught the first school, which was on Sulphur Fork. About 1805, Thomas Bowles and John Edwards taught at Springfield, and in the next year, according to N. W. True, Liberty Academy was established at Springfield. This became a noted school, and many prominent men were educated there. It existed about seventy-five years and was then sold to some Negroes who used it for a church.

Early churches were the Red River Missionary Baptist Church, the first, 1791; the Cane Ridge Presbyterian Church, 1793, where some of the services of the great revival of 1800 were held, and Mount Zion. A large camp ground was maintained also.

This county was the home of the so-called Bell Witch about whom hair-raising stories were told, and also of the octoroon Elijah Cheek. It was also the scene of some of the startling exploits of the Night Riders a few years ago.

Statistics of Robertson County: population, 1920, 25,621. Assessed valuation of taxable property, 1921, $17,859,694. Area, 536 square miles. Number of farms, 4,002. Railway mileage, 26. Surface is hilly and well covered with timber. The soil is fertile. Tobacco is one of the principal products, this county being one of the largest producers in the state. Other staple products are wheat, corn, oats, and live stock. Springfield, the county seat, has a population of 3,860 and is a flourishing town. It is one of the chief tobacco markets of the state. Springfield is on the L. & N. Railroad and is 30 miles from Nashville. It has fine schools and churches, two weekly newspapers, four banks, and manufacturing establishments. Adams, Green Brier, and Cedar Hill are other towns. Scholastic population of county, 9,393; high schools, 9; elementary schools, 74.

RUTHERFORD COUNTY

RUTHERFORD COUNTY was erected on October 25, 1803, from Davidson County and was named in honor of Gen. Griffith Rutherford, of North Carolina. It was organized on January 3, 1803.

Uriah Stone, who discovered Stone's River, in 1766, explored it as far as Old Jefferson in Rutherford County. The famous Indian chief, Black Fox, had a camp near Murfreesboro and the old Indian war trace from Nashville to Chattanooga passed through this county.

Early settlers were: Sam Wilson, who located at Wilson's

Shoals on Stone's River; William Adkinson, Thomas Nelson, and Thomas Howell, near Stewart Creek; Robert Overall, on Overall Creek; Nimrod Menifee, near the Federal Cemetery; Col. Robert Weakley, Robert Bedford, Col. Richard Ransom, Rev. James Bowman, Charles Ready, Thomas Rucker, Richard Saunders, and Capt. William Lytle, the last named being the owner of the land on the site of Murfreesboro.

On August 3, 1804, the commissioners, John Hill, Frederick Barfield, Mark Mitchell, Alexander McBride, and Peter Legrand, selected a county seat. Through the influence of Col. Robert Weakley and Robert Bedford they selected Jefferson, known now as Old Jefferson, on land between the forks of Stone's River. The first court was held at the house of Thomas Rucks on January 3, 1804, and the first courthouse was erected in 1804-1805. Parry W. Humphreys was made county solicitor. Thomas H. Benton tried his first case at Jefferson.

On October 17, 1811, the Legislature directed that a county seat be determined and named and appointed seven prominent land owners to select a site of sixty acres, centrally located. A struggle ensued between rival factions. The site was first called Cannonsburg in honor of Newton Cannon, governor 1835-1839, but by an amendment to the act of 1811 it was called Murfreesborough in honor of Col. Hardy Murfree, who led the advance at the battle of Stony Point and was incorporated on October 17, 1817. The first mayor was Joshua Haskell, who resigned and was succeeded by Joseph Wendell. Lawyers of early days were: S. R. Rucker, J. R. Martin, Charles Ready, S. A. Laughlin, W. Brady, Samuel Anderson, John Bruce, Joshua Haskell, and P. W. Humphreys. Early physicians were: Drs. James Mooney, J. King, Henry Holmes, and P. Yandell.

The Tennessee Legislature held its session in Murfreesboro from 1819-1826, its meetings being in the courthouse.

Important educational institutions: Soule College, originally Soule's Female Academy, founded in 1825; Old Union University, chartered February 5, 1842; Tennessee College; Anderson's School for Boys; and the Middle Tennessee Normal School.

Murfreesboro has been the home of two great literary celebrities: Dr. Samuel P. Baldwin, author of "Armageddon," and Miss Mary N. Murfree (George Egbert Craddock), whose lamented death occurred recently.

Statistics of Rutherford County: population, 1920, 33,059. Assessed valuation of taxable property, 1921, $25,441,330.

Area, 580 square miles. Number of farms, 5,254. Railway Mileage, 34. Drained by Stone's River, a tributary of the Cumberland River. Its surface is undulating, and the soil is fertile. Portions of the county are well timbered. Staple products are corn, cotton, wheat, sorghum, peas, clover, and grass. It is one of the best live-stock counties in the state. Murfreesboro, the county seat, has a population of 5,367 and is on the N. C. & St. L. Railway, 30 miles from Nashville. It has fine public and private schools and is the seat of the Middle Tennessee Normal. It has splendid churches, two weekly newspapers, several manufacturing establishments, and prosperous stores. Christiana, Fosterville, Smyrna, and LaVergne are other towns in the county. Scholastic population of county, 14,367; high schools, 15; elementary schools, 100.

SMITH COUNTY

SMITH COUNTY was erected in 1799 from a part of Sumner County and was named in honor of Gen. Daniel Smith, a pioneer, surveyor, Secretary of the Southwest Territory, and United States Senator, succeeding Andrew Jackson.

The early settlers were mostly from North Carolina and Virginia, some of them via East Tennessee. They raised cotton, corn, tobacco, and hemp. William Walton was the first settler, having located, probably in 1787, on what was afterwards the site of Carthage. Other early settlers were: Daniel Burford, Richard Alexander, Peter Turney, William Saunders, Tilman Dixon, Micajah Duke, William McDonald, William Goodall, Armstead Flippin, James Hodges, George T. Wright, Arthur S. Hogan, the Gordons, Smiths, and Fites.

On December 16, 1799, the first session of the Court of Pleas and Quarter Sessions was held at the house of Tilman Dixon on the site of Dixon Springs. The following-named magistrates were present and qualified: Garrett Fitzgerald, chairman, William Alexander, James Gwinn, Tilman Dixon, Thos. Harrison, James Hibbetts, William Walton, and Peter Turney. The last named was the father of Hopkins L. Turney and grandfather of Governor Peter Turney. The oath was administered by Moses Fisk, who was appointed clerk, pro tem. Amos Lacy was chosen constable. During its first year this court had its meetings sometimes at the house of Maj. Dixon and sometimes at William Saunders', then at Fort Blount, then at Colonel Walton's. But in 1804, the county site was established at the place where Carthage now stands, which was laid out on the land of Col. William Walton, who built the road, called after him, the Walton Road, from the junction of the Caney Fork and the Cumberland across the mountain, along which road he erected houses for the entertainment of travelers. The courthouse was completed in 1805, and in March, 1806, the court was held in it.

The circuit court held its first session, it is thought, in 1810, with Judge N. W. Williams presiding. The chancery court held its first term in May, 1825, and was presided over by Judge John Catron, Chief Justice of the state, 1831-1835, and then member of the United States Supreme Court. Among the prominent members of its bar were: Robert L. Caruthers, elected governor in 1863, and his brother, Abraham Caruthers, William B. Campbell, governor, 1851-1853, William Cullom, Samuel M. Fite, James B. Moore, Jordan Stokes, John D. Goodall, Andrew McClain, A. A. Swope, E. L. Gardenhire, and Sam Turney.

Smith County furnished for the War of 1812 two companies whose captains were, respectively, Robertson and James Walton; four companies for the War with Mexico, commanded by Captains William Walton, L. P. McMurry, Don Allison, and John D. Goodall; and twelve companies to the Confederate Army.

Pioneer ministers were: David P. Timberlake, David Halliburton, John Page, Jesse Moreland, and John Maffit.

Important educational institutions were the Geneva Academy and the Female Academy.

Statistics of Smith County: population of 1920, 17,134. Assessed valuation of taxable property, 1923, $13,652,578. Area, 368 square miles. Number of farms, 2,908. Railway mileage, 27. Drained by the Cumberland and its tributary, the Caney Fork. Surface is hilly and well covered with timber. Staple products are corn, wheat, oats, tobacco, and hay. It is one of the best live stock counties in the state. Carthage, the county seat, is on the Cumberland River and the terminus of a branch of the Tennessee Central Railway. It has a population of 920, has good schools and churches, a weekly newspaper, one bank, manufacturing and mercantile establishments. Large shipments of tobacco are made from Carthage. Dixon Springs is another prosperous town in the county. Scholastic population of county, 6,832; high schools, 2; elementary schools, 72.

STEWART COUNTY

STEWART COUNTY was erected on November 1, 1803, from a part of Montgomery County and was named in honor of Duncan Stewart, an energetic and prosperous farmer. At that time this county included a vast domain extending west to the Tennessee River and south to the Alabama line. After the Chickasaw purchase was made, October 19, 1918, the jurisdiction of this county for a while extended to the Mississippi River and covered more than 1,200 square miles, more than one-fourth of the entire state.

The earliest settlers arrived about 1795, mostly from North Carolina. Among them were: George Petty, Samuel A. Smith, Britton Sexton, James Andrews, Samuel Boyd, and Elisha Dawson. They settled on or near the site of Dover. About 1800 Duncan Stewart arrived with a large number of immigrants from North Carolina. Among them were: John Kingins, Christopher Brandon, Joseph Smith, Tillman Sexton, and Ethelred Wallace. In 1809 and 1811, John Wofford and James Wofford came. From Virginia came: James Scarborough, Sr., James Scarborough, Jr., Davis Andrews, and Ebenezer Rumphelt. Other pioneer families were: the Lewis, Gorham, Weaks, Parchman, Walter, and Akers families.

Most of the settlers from North Carolina had grants of land for services in the Revolutionary War. For several years they suffered much from the depredations of the Indians.

On November 1st, 1803, the Legislature passed an act in which a commission was appointed to select the county seat. The county was organized on March 12, 1804, at the house of George Martin, near Bald Island, by the following-named magistrates: Thomas Clinton, Joshua Williams, William Allen, and George Petty.

In 1805 thirty acres were bought of Robert Nelson and a county seat laid out. Although the act creating the county specified that the name of the county seat should be Monroe, it was nevertheless called Dover. It was incorporated in 1836.

Among the early lawyers who practiced at Dover were: Nathaniel McNairy, Jesse E. Rice, H. C. Roberts, James Roberts, Percy W. Thompson, Aaron Goodridge, E. P. Petty, J. B. Reynolds, J. W. Wall, C. M. Brandon, J. W. Rice, M. Brandon, Jesse L. Harris, J. O. Shackleford, Peter Lynch, Hiram Valentine, John Reddick, William Fitzgerald, West H. Humphreys, George W. Marr.

Early physicians were: Drs. Brunson, Huling, Cato, Outlaw, and Roberts.

Probably the first school was taught by John Ferrell in

1806. Alexander Coppage was a noted teacher of 1826. In 1840, McDougal opened a "Male and Female Academy."

The Baptists established the first church probably in 1803.

From 1854 to 1856 a servile insurrection, probably the only one in the history of Tennessee was fomented in this county, supposedly by white preachers. The plan was for the Negroes to overcome their masters on a certain day and then to leave for Ohio where they expected to be freed. In December, 1856, the plot was discovered by the vigilance committee. Six of the leaders were hanged and many were whipped.

Stewart County was for more than fifty years the center of the iron industry of Middle Tennessee.

Statistics of Stewart County: population, 1920, 14,664. Assessed valuation of taxable property, 1921, $5,520,099. Area, 500 square miles. Number of farms, 2,612. Railway mileage, 5. Drained by the Cumberland River which intersects the county. The Tennessee River flows along the western border of the county. Its surface is hilly and partly covered with timber. The soil is fertile. A large amount of export tobacco is grown. Other staple products are corn, wheat, oats, and live stock. Several iron mines have been worked in the county. The L. & N. Railroad passes through the county. Dover, the county seat, has a population of about 500 and has good schools and churches, weekly newspaper, two banks, and flourishing business houses. Scholastic population of county, 5,576; high schools, 1; elementary schools, 63.

SUMNER COUNTY*

SUMNER COUNTY was erected on November 17, 1786, by act of the Legislature of North Carolina. It was formed from a part of Davidson County and was named in honor of Gen. Jethro Sumner, a gallant officer in the Revolutionary War. It was the second county formed in Middle Tennessee.

Cisco says, "The curtain of history arises on Sumner County in the year 1779, when a settlement of a dozen families was formed near Bledsoe's Lick," now Castalian Springs. Before this day, however, Thomas Sharp Spencer and others had come into the Cumberland country and in 1777 had built a number of cabins about one-half mile west of Bledsoe's Lick, and in 1778 had planted some corn. This was the first agricultural effort made by men of the Anglo-Saxon race in Middle Tennessee.

*The historical facts in the sketch of this county have been taken largely from Cisco's Historic Sumner County.

Col. Isaac Bledsoe built a fort or station about a quarter of a mile west of Bledsoe's Lick; and his brother, Col. Anthony Bledsoe, built a fort two and one-half miles north of the Lick and called it "Greenfield."

Asher and others built a fort a little southeast of Gallatin. Forts were also built by John Morgan, Maj. James White, Colonel Sanders, Jacob Zigler, Capt. Jos. Wilson, ancestor of Judge S. F. Wilson,* of the State Court of Chancery Appeals, Kasper Mansker, Hamilton, and others.

Among the early settlers were: Col. Isaac Bledsoe, Col. Anthony Bledsoe, Robert Desha, Jordon Gibson, Henry Loving, William Morrison, John Morgan, John Sawyer, Robert Steele, Jacob Zeigler, Henry Ramsey, William Hall, Hugh Rogan, David Shelby, George D. Blackmore, James and George Winchester, Robert Peyton, Jos. Wilson, Michael Shafer, James Hayes, Charles Morgan, Gabriel Black, John Carr, Robert Brigham, Charles Campbell, William Crawford, Edward and Elmore Douglass, James Franklin, Richard Hogan, Robert and David Looney, George Mansker, Benjamin Kuykendall, Thomas Sharp Spencer, John Peyton, James McCain, Benjamin Porter, John Withers, John Hamilton, John Latham, William Snoddy, James Cartwright, James McCann, John and Joseph Byrns, James Trousdale, Benjamin Williams, John Edwards, Samuel Wilson, John Hall, William Montgomery, Edward Hagan, Gen. Daniel Smith, William Frazier, Benjamin Sheppard, and Redmond D. Berry, who introduced Kentucky bluegrass and brought from North Carolina his blooded horse, Gray Metley.

The first court of Sumner County was held on the first Monday in March, 1787, at the house of John Hamilton, at Station Camp Creek, about five miles from Gallatin. The members of that court were: Gen. Daniel Smith, Maj. David Wilson, Maj. George Winchester, Isaac Lindsey, William Hall, John Hardin, Joseph Kuykendall, Col. Edward Douglass, and Col. Isaac Bledsoe. David Shelby, son-in-law of Col. Anthony Bledsoe, was appointed clerk. John Hardin, Jr., was appointed sheriff, and Isaac Lindsey, ranger.

On April 20, 1796, the Legislature of Tennessee passed an act appointing commissioners to select a site for the seat of government. Those commissioners were: William Bowen, John Wilson, Isaac Walton, George D. Blackmore, and Hugh Crawford. The act also appointed the following trustees to purchase the land selected by the commissioners: Henry Bradford, David Shelby, and Edward Douglas. Section 3 of this act provided that the town should be called "Ca Ira," which name was corrupted into "Cairo," and it was so incorporated on November 5, 1815. On October 2, 1797, this act was repealed and another act passed appointing another commission to select the county site, to buy land, erect a courthouse, prison, and stocks.

This act also was repealed on October 26, 1799, and Sumner County was reduced to its constitutional limits. On November 6, 1804, an act was passed by the Legislature to provide for county seat and buildings and that the town should be called Gallatin, in honor of Albert Gallatin, Secretary of the Treasury of the United States.

In February, 1802, the site of Gallatin was purchased from James Trousdale. The courthouse was completed in 1803.

The circuit court was established in 1810, and the chancery court in 1836. The sessions of the Court of Pleas and Quarter Sessions were held in the homes of various citizens until the courthouse was erected. The first session of the court after Tennessee was admitted into the Union was held in the house of Ezekiel Douglas in July, 1796. It was composed of the following members appointed by Governor Sevier: William Cage, Stephen Cantrell, James Douglass, Edward Douglass, James Gwyn, Wetheral Lattimore, Thomas Masten, Thomas Donald, James Pearce, David Wilson, James Winchester, and Isaac Walton. Probably from eighty to one hundred persons in Sumner County were killed by the Indians. An academy for girls was incorporated November 3, 1837. It was succeeded by the Howard Female Institute in 1856. Joseph S. Fowler was a teacher in this school. After the war he became a Senator of the United States from Tennessee. It was his vote which saved Andrew Johnson from being convicted when impeached.

Early ministers from the county were: John Gwynn, James McGhee, Bishop McKendree, John Page, Methodists; John Wiseman, Baptist; William McGhee, Presbyterian.

Statistics of Sumner County: population, 1920, 27,708. Assessed valuation of taxable property, 1921, $21,557,328. Area, 536 square miles. Number of farms, 4,585. Railway mileage, 62. Sumner County is one of the finest stock-raising and agricultural section in the state and is intersected by the L. & N. Railroad, borders on Kentucky, and is bounded on the south by the Cumberland River. Portions of it are well timbered and it is a fine county for fruit-growing. Phosphate deposits are found in the county. It has a good system of highways. Staple products are corn, wheat, tobacco, hay, and live stock. Gallatin, the county seat, is on the L. & N. Railroad and is 30 miles from Nashville and has fine schools and churches, two weekly newspapers, two banks, and prosperous manufacturing and mercantile establishments. Gallatin has a population of 2,757. Portland is another prosperous town. Scholastic population of county, 9,672; high schools, 13; elementary schools, 83.

TROUSDALE COUNTY

TROUSDALE COUNTY was erected in 1870 from parts of Sumner, Macon, Smith, and Wilson County and was named in honor of William Trousdale, Governor, 1849-1851.

The first court was held in the Methodist Church at Hartsville on the first Monday in September, 1870. The following-named magistrates were present: James R. DeBow, chairman, Charles McMurray, and James R. Jefferies. Hartsville was chosen as the county seat in an election held in the following November. The circuit court held its first term in September, 1870, Judge W. H. Williamson presiding.

The following chancellors have presided over the division of which Trousdale County is a part: Charles G. Smith, Horace H. Lurton, afterwards a member of the United States Supreme Court, B. J. Tarver, and George H. Seay.

The Lauderdale, Donoho, Sewell, Cunningham, Mill, and Caruthers families were early settlers in this county. Albert Gallatin Donoho was the first white child born near Hartsville, in 1798. Like the people in all the neighboring counties, the early settlers here suffered much from the atrocities of the Indians.

The section afterwards known as Trousdale County sent a company to the Mexican War under command of Capt. R. A. Bennett and Lieutenants J. M. Shaver, Patrick Duffy, and King Kirby.

Among its distinguished officers in the War between the States were: Col. James Bennett, Capt. William Barksdale, Maj. G. Lowe, Capt. H. C. Ellis, and Col. William J. Hale.

The battle of Hartsville was fought on December 7, 1862. The Federal garrison, after an hour's fight, surrendered to the Confederates under Gen. John Morgan.

Statistics of Trousdale County: population, 1920, 5,996. Assessed valuation of taxable property, 1921, $5,369,678. Area, 166 square miles. Number of farms, 876. Railway mileage, 8. Drained by Cumberland River and its tributaries. Surface is hilly with rich valleys and splendidly adapted to stock-raising.

Staple products are corn, wheat, tobacco, hay, and live stock. Hartsville, the county seat, is on the Cumberland River and the terminus of a branch of the L. & N. Railroad. It has a population of 1,023 and has good schools and churches, a weekly newspaper, two banks, and prosperous business establishments. Scholastic population of county, 1,734; high schools, 1; elementary schools, 25.

VAN BUREN COUNTY

VAN BUREN COUNTY was erected in 1840 from parts of White, Warren, and Bledsoe Counties and named for Martin Van Buren, who was President at that time. The first court was held on April 6, 1840, at Spencer, named for Thomas Sharp Spencer, who was killed by the Indians in this county.

Burritt College, at Spencer, was established in the fifties, with accommodations for 250 students. Its influence on education in this section has been incalculable.

Statistics of Van Buren County: population, 1920, 2,624. Assessed valuation of taxable property, 1921, $1,693,762. Area, 322 square miles. Number of farms, 432. Railway mileage, none. This county is well drained and has much fine timber and fine grazing lands for cattle and sheep. Staple products are corn, grasses, fruits, and live stock. Spencer, the county seat, has a population of about 300 and has good schools and churches, a bank, and prosperous business establishments. Scholastic population of county, 1,013. High schools, 1; elementary schools, 21.

WARREN COUNTY

WARREN COUNTY was erected in 1807 from a part of White County and is said to have been named for Gen. William Warren, who fell at the battle of Bunker Hill. It is believed that Elisha Pepper, who came from Virginia about 1800, was the first settler. Other early settlers were: Joseph Colville, John Lusk, Lyon Mitchell, William Lusk, Dr. John Wilson, Edward Hogue, Dr. W. P. Lawrence, Absalom Clark, Elijah Fletcher, John England, Irwin Hill, Oliver Charles, Abner Womack, William Womack, Chesley Webb, John Kirby, Robert Biles, Archibald Prater, Allen Youngblood, Brown Spurlock, Thomas Gribble, Mason French, James Northcutt, William Smartt, Dr. Archibald Faulkner,

Asa Faulkner, John Gross, James Cape, William Cummings, Joshua Hickerson, Oliver Charles, H. J. A. Hill, W. J. Stubblefield, John Davis, and James Elkins.

Until 1810 the courts were held at the home of Joseph Westmoreland and in a log house near it about a half mile south of Barren Fork. This was near the celebrated Poplar Tavern where people intending to settle on Elk River usually stopped. In March, 1809, McMinnville was selected as the county seat by the commissioners, James Taylor, Thomas Matthews, Benjamin Lockhart, James English, and John Armstrong. It was located on the lands of Joseph Colville, John A. Wilson, and Robert Cowan. In August, 1810, McMinnville was laid off and lots sold.

Among the early lawyers were: T. V. Murray, Washington Brittain, George Stubblefield, John B. Forester, William Armstrong, Stokeley D. Rowan, Andrew J. Marchbanks, Napoleon B. Baird, B. L. Ridley, Thomas K. Harris.

This county has furnished soldiers for all the wars in which Tennessee has had a part.

Early educational institutions were: Quincy Academy, founded in 1809; Edmondson Academy, established in 1820; Carroll Academy, in 1830; and the Cumberland Female College, in 1850.

Early churches were: Shiloh and Sulphur Springs Churches, both Union and Hickory Grove, Methodist. The Primitive Baptist Church was the first church established in McMinnville in 1837. Rev. Isaac Woodward, a saintly and eccentric Methodist, was the best known of the pioneer ministers.

Dr. J. P. Lawrence was one of the first physicians.

Statistics of Warren County: population, 1920, 17,306. Assessed valuation of taxable property, 1921, $7,715,632. Area, 440 square miles. Number of farms, 2,756. Railway mileage, 25. Drained by the Caney Fork and Rock Rivers. Surface is hilly with fertile valleys—splendid fruit-growing section. Some sections are well timbered. Staple products are corn, wheat, oats, and live stock. A branch of the N. C. & St. L. Railway intersects the county. McMinnville, the county seat, has a population of 2,814 and is a flourishing town with fine schools and churches, a weekly newspaper, three banks, manufacturing establishments, and prosperous stores, flour mills, saw mills, etc. Morrison and Rock Island are other towns. Scholastic population of county, 5,760, high schools, 7; elementary schools, 66.

WAYNE COUNTY

WAYNE COUNTY was erected by act of the Legislature on November 24, 1817, from parts of Hickman and Humphreys Counties and named in honor of Gen. Anthony Wayne. This act, however, was not engrossed and approved and, therefore, had to be repassed at the session of 1819.

The first meeting for organization of the county court was held at the house of Benjamin Hardin, on the Factor's fork of Shoal Creek at the crossing of the Natchez Trace. The next meeting was held at William Barnett's on the Old Town Branch where Barnett had built a log courthouse, and the following magistrates were present: Benjamin Hardin, Jesse Cypert, William B. Curtis, William Burns, Perley and David Gallaher, Reuben Kyle, John Meredith, C. W. Pope, William B. Ross, Henry Rayburn, and William B. Walker.

The county officers elected were: William Barnett, county court clerk; Benjamin Hardin, sheriff; John M. Barnett, circuit court clerk; John McClure, register; John Meredith, trustee; John Hill, ranger; and W. B. Payne, coroner.

Courts were held at this place until 1823, when the county seat was moved to Waynesboro, which was founded by William Burns, in 1821, and was sold by him to the commissioners appointed to locate the county seat, viz: Nathan Biffer, Charles Burns, James Hollis, and John Hill. This land, forty acres, was divided into lots, which were sold and proceeds used to erect a courthouse.

The first chancery court was held at Waynesboro in 1847, Judge Terry H. Cahal presiding, C. B. McLean, clerk and master.

The mineral deposits of the county are extensive. The iron deposits have been and are still being worked. There are also important deposits of maganese and cement.

Wayne and Hardin Counties are two of the best wooded counties in the state.

The first schools, Ashland Academy, was built at Waynesboro in 1843. In 1849 the Female Academy was established at the same place.

The Masonic Academy was built at Clifton in 1855 and Frank Hughes College also at Clifton in 1906.

The first settlement was made on Pine River by Adam Wilson.

Statistics of Wayne County: population, 1920, 12,877. Assessed valuation of taxable property, 1921, $4,232,812. Area, 720 square miles. Number of farms, 1,651. Railway mileage,

18. Drained by tributaries of the Tennessee River. Surface generally hilly and is a splendid fruit-growing section. A large part of the county is well timbered. Staple products are corn, wheat, cotton, hay, and live stock. Limestone and iron ore are found in the county. Waynesboro, the county seat, has a population of about 600 and has good schools and churches, bank, and prosperous business establishments. Collinwood, another town, has large manufacturing interests. Scholastic population of county, 5,220; high schools, 4; elementary schools, 71.

WHITE COUNTY

WHITE COUNTY was erected on September 11, 1806, from a part of Smith County and was named for John White, one of the first settlers in this county. The first settlements were made in the valley of the Calf Killer River, so named for an Indian Chief. Among the early settlers were: John White, Elijah Camerson, William Phillips, John Knowles, Archibald Overton, Aaron England, William Scarborough, Isaac Taylor, Alexander Lowery, George W. Gibbs, John Hancock, T. B. Rice, Joseph Terry, Anthony Dibrell, Jacob A. Lane, Thomas Simpson, William Anderson, Matthais Anderson, Benjamin Lampton, Lewis Fletcher, Thomas Bounds, Jesse Lincoln, William Glenn, William Burton, Joseph Collins, Montgomery Carrick.

The first court was held at the house of Joseph Terry, on the present site of Rock Island, in Warren County, on October 15, 1806.

In 1809 the Legislature passed an act for the establishment of Sparta, the county seat, and the following commissioners were elected to lay it off: Thomas Bounds, Benjamin Weaver, Aaron England, Turner Lane, James Fulkerson Alexander Lowry, and Nicholas Gillentine.

The first courthouse was built of logs in 1810 and stood until 1815 when a brick building was erected, which was used until 1894, when a new building was constructed.

For several years the superior court met in White County, at first at Rock Island, and later at Sparta.

Among the early lawyers were: Alexander Lane, David Ames, Nathaniel Hoggard, Richard Nelson, John H. Anderson, Hopkins L. Turney, Sam Turney, John Catron, and George W. Gibbs.

The first representative in Congress from White County was Thomas K. Harris. He was killed in a duel with Col. John

W. Simpson at Shell's Ford on Caney Fork River. Prior to this unfortunate occurrence, Col. Simpson had distinguished himself at the battle of New Orleans as had Captain Gibbs, also of White County.

White County also furnished troops for the Creek War, the War with Mexico, and the War between the States.

About 1815 a turnpike road built from Nashville to Knoxville passed through Sparta.

The mineral wealth of White County, especially coal, is remarkable. In 1882 the Bon Air Coal, Land & Lumber Company was organized by Gen. George G. Dibrell and his associates, ex-Governor John C. Brown, Col. John F. House, Gen. J. D. Adkins, Gen. W. C. Whitthorne, Hon. Benton McMillin, then a member of Congress, Dr. W. M. Morrow, D. W. Dinges, Samuel G. Jones, and W. C. Dibrell.

Statistics of White County: population, 1920, 15,701. Assessed valuation of taxable property, 1921, $7,845,005. Area, 390 square miles. Number of farms, 2,024. Railway mileage, 36. Drained by the Caney Fork River. The surface is uneven and extensively covered with timber. The soil is fertile. The staple products are corn, wheat, oats, and live stock. Good fruit-growing section. The Bon Air Coal Mines are located in this county. A branch of the Nashville, Chattanooga & St. Louis Railway extends into the county. Sparta, the county seat, with a population of 1,517, is on the railroad and is a town of good schools and churches, a weekly newspaper, two banks, and manufacturing and commercial establishments, electric light and power plant. Scholastic population of county, 5,869; high schools, 3; elementary schools, 56.

WILLIAMSON COUNTY*

THE act creating Williamson County was passed on October 26, 1799. It was formed from Davidson County and, according to Dr. W. M. Clarke, named for "General Williamson, of North Carolina, some of whose descendants were prominent men of that day; among others, Dr. Hugh Williamson, the intimate friend and companion of Franklin. It is supposed by some that the county received its name from

---

*The historical facts in this sketch are taken partly from Park Marshall's History of Franklin and Williamson Counties, published serially in the Williamson County News. Mr. Marshall made a scrapbook of the clippings which he presented to the State on November 18, 1919.

Dr. Williamson and the county seat from the name of his eminent friend."†

Hunters and explorers went into Williamson County as early as 1784, and the Harpeth (spelled at first Harpath) was known in that same year. Permanent settlements, however, were not made until shortly before 1800, on account of fear of the Indians. Probably the first permanent settlement was made in 1798 by several families headed by David McEwen, who located at Roper's Knob. At nearly the same time William Demonbreun, son of the famous Timothy Demonbreun, settled at College Grove. A pioneer named Sledge settled near Paytonsville.

Among the numerous pioneers who settled in this county from 1797 to 1810 may be mentioned Stephen Childress, Nicholas Perkins, Byrd Bramlett, Edmund Wall, John Harness, R. P. Currin, Robert Caruthers, Zion Hunt, William Hulme, Solomen Brent, Abram Maury, Thos. McKay, Ewen Cameron,‡ William Edmondston, Matthew Johnson, Thomas H. Perkins, George Neely, Andrew Goff, John Fulson, and Samuel Crockett.

The act of October 26, 1799, provided "that Abraham Maury, John Walthall, Joseph Porter, William Boyd, and David McEwen are hereby constituted and appointed commissioners for the regulation of said town of Franklin, vested with full power and authority for that purpose, provided they govern themselves by the original plan of said town."

This plan was filed in the clerk's office April 5, 1800. The court of Pleas and Quarter Sessions held its first meeting on February 3, the first Monday in February, 1800, at the house of Thomas McKay on the site of Franklin and continued to meet there until November 3, 1800, when and afterwards its sessions were held at the courthouse. The magistrates present at the first meeting were: John Johnson, Sr., James Buford, James Scurlock, Chapman White, and Daniel Perkins. Scurlock was elected chairman, but resigned and was succeeded by White.

The first courthouse was probably on the square. Being a poor structure, it was succeeded by a new courthouse authorized by the General Assembly on September 11, 1806. This courthouse was erected in the center of the public square. Among the lawyers practicing in Franklin in the early days were: Thomas H. Benton, John H. Eaton, Seth Lewis, Jesse Wharton, I. Johnston, L. P. Montgomery, Joseph Herndon,

---
†Killebrew's Resources of Tennessee, page 991.
‡It is said that he erected the first house in Franklin in 1797.

John Dickinson, John McNutt, William Smith, Bennett Searcy, P. W. Humphreys, G. W. L. Mann, Peter R. Booker, Felix Grundy.

The circuit court was authorized by the Legislature on November 16, 1809. Thomas Stewart was Circuit Judge from November, 1811 to 1836. The first solicitor before this court was Alfred Balch.

Among the notable cases tried in the Franklin Court was the "Crenshaw case." Daniel Crenshaw was indicted in 1826 for stealing a horse from Robert C. Foster and a gray mare from Kersiah Wooldridge, also for forgery. He was defended by John Bell and pleaded "Benefit of Clergy," thereby escaping punishment in two cases.

Another notable case was the trial of David Perry and Jonathan Magness for the killing of Patten Anderson, the friend of Andrew Jackson.

Williamson County is rich in the number of prominent and famous men who have lived there. Among them the following deserve special mention: Thomas H. Benton, whose mother moved from North Carolina to occupy a tract of forty thousand acres a few miles from Franklin. From 1808 to 1812 he had more cases at the Franklin bar than any other lawyer.

John Bell, born in Nashville, was sworn in as an attorney in Franklin in 1816 at the age of nineteen.

Meredith P. Gentry, one of the greatest of Tennessee orators, Rev. Gideon Blackburn, a minister in Franklin from 1811 to 1822.

In 1825 the following-named distinguished lawyers were practicing at the Franklin bar: Felix Grundy, George W. Campbell, John Bell, G. S. Yerger, William Hadley, W. S. Hunt, John Thompson, William McGee, William Thompson, A. P. Maury, M. W. Campbell, David Craighead, P. S. Daily, Andrew Hays, Sam Houston, Robert C. Foster, N. P. Smith, C. S. Olmstead, Thomas Washington, James P. Clark, Jesse Greer, and N. P. Perkins.

The important educational institutions were: Harpeth Academy, chartered in 1807, and the buildings sold to Randall McGavock in 1823; Harpeth Union Female Academy established in 1828; Tennessee Female College; and Battle Ground Academy.

The battle of Franklin which, when the forces engaged are considered, was the bloodiest of the war was fought on November 30th, 1864.

Statistics of Williamson County: population, 1920, 23,409. Assessed valuation of taxable property, 1921, $22,529,433.

Area, 550 square miles. Number of farms, 3,355. Railway mileage, 60. Drained by Harpeth River. Surface is rolling and very fertile with fine growth of timber. Wheat, oats, corn, cotton, and live stock are staple products. Franklin, the county seat, twenty miles from Nashville, on the L. & N. Railroad, has a population of 3,123, good schools and churches, two weekly newspapers, three banks, and manufacturing and commercial establishments. Extensive deposits of phosphate are found in this county. Scholastic population, 10,192; high schools, 10; elementary schools, 89.

WILSON COUNTY

WILSON COUNTY and Smith County were erected on the same day, October 26, 1799, from a part of Sumner County. Wilson County was named for Maj. David Wilson, a native of Pennsylvania, who came to Sumner while it was yet a part of North Carolina and had been the first Speaker of the Territorial Assembly.

The first court of the county was held on December 23, 1799, at the house* of Capt. John Harpool (or Harpole) and was organized by the following-named magistrates: Charles Cavenaugh, John Alcorn, John Lancaster, Elmore Douglas, John Doak, Matthew Figures, Henry Ross, William Gray, Andrew Donelson, and William McClain. The following-named officers were elected: Charles Cavenaugh, chairman; Robert Foster, clerk; Charles Rosborough, sheriff; William Gray, ranger; and John Alcorn, register. Ben Seawell, Esq., was appointed county solicitor, and John C. Hamilton qualified as a practicing attorney.

The first settlement in the county was at Drake's Lick on the Cumberland River and was made in 1797 by John Foster and William McClain. In 1799 a settlement was made on Spring Creek, seven miles southeast of Lebanon by John Foster, William Donnell, and Alexander Barkley (or Barclay). In the same year a settlement was made at Round Lick by Samuel King, James Rather, William McSpadden, and William Harris, and on Spring Creek eight or nine miles south of Lebanon by David Magathey, Foster Doak, John Doak, Alexander Braden, and the Donnells.

After 1800 immigrants came in constantly in increasing numbers. Robin Shannon, Lee Harrelson, John Ozment, John Spinks, John Rice, and others settled at Pond Lick, Jacob

*Probably on Spring Creek, five miles north of Lebanon.

Vantrease, Thomas B. Reece, John Caplinger, Edmund Jennings, John Patton, George Hearn, James Edwards, Duncan Johnson, Daniel Smith, Isaac Grandstaff, Evans Tracy, William Neal, Shelah Waters, Joseph Barbee, Solomon Bass, John Lawrence, Jordan Bass, John Green, William Coe, John Phillips, William Haines, Arthur Hawkins, Benjamin Phillips, and John W. Peyton located at Round Lick; Martin Talley, William Sherrill, Pernell Hearn, James Cannon, John Jones, Benjamin Mottley, Henry Chandler, Adair Harpole, and Gregory Johnson, on Spring Creek; Robert Jarmon, Lewis Merritt, David Fields, Jonathan Ozment, Dawson Hancock, and Seldon Baird, on Sinking Creek; Absalom Knight, John Gibson, Charles Cummings, Henry Mosier, John Merritt, Frank Young, Joseph Stacey, and Charles Warren, on Hurricane Creek; Frank Puckett, William Lester, John Donnell, Lord Sellers, John Alsup, Aaron Edwards, Sampson Smith, Jacob Jennings, and William Warren, on Fall Creek; Hooker Reeves, Joseph Weir, Lewis Chambers, Nathan Cartwright, William Wilson, Matthew Figures, on Cedar Creek; Joseph Castleman, Joseph Hamilton, Thomas Drennon, Benjamin Dobson, Aquila Suggs, and Benjamin Hooker, on Suggs' Creek; Clement Jennings, James H. Davis, Thomas Davis, Joshua Kelley, Harrison Hays, Theophilas Bass, on Cedar Lick Creek; George L. Smith, William Oakley, Charles Rich, Reason Byrne, Abner Bone, James McAdoo, Edward Pickett, John Adams, David Ireland, on Smith Ford; Caleb Taylor, James Hunter, Joseph Kirkpatrick, Daniel Glenn, Sterling Tarpley, and William Saunders, on the Cumberland River.

The first white male child born in the county was probably Josiah McClain, who was county court clerk for more than forty years.

Lawyers who practiced in the courts of Wilson County in the first years were: Jesse Wharton, Nicholas Perkins, John B. Johnson, Lemuel Herrod, John Dickinson, Charles Smith.

In 1802 the court was held at the house of Henry Turner on Barton Creek.

Lebanon was chosen as the county seat in 1802 and was located on land previously belonging to James Menees. It was named for the Biblical Lebanon because, like the ancient city, it was remarkable for its cedars. It was incorporated in 1807. Neddie Jacobs, a peculiar character and a fiddler, was the first settler on this site. Tradition says he was living there as early as 1800. The earliest physicians were: Drs. Samuel Hogg, Edmund Crutcher, and Henry Shelley. Dr. Shelley built the first brick house in Lebanon in 1812. John

Alcorn was the first postmaster and John Trotter the first school teacher. The first church was erected by the Methodists in 1802 and Rev. German Baker was the pastor.

From December, 1802 to 1806, the Court of Pleas and Quarter Sessions met at private houses. In 1806 the first courthouse, of cedar logs, was built.

The first session of the circuit court was held at the courthouse on September 24, 1810, Judge Thomas Stewart presiding. Early circuit judges were: Thomas Stewart, 1810-1830; James C. Mitchell, 1830-1835; Samuel Anderson, 1835-1852.

Lebanon and Wilson County have been justly celebrated for educational facilities from the establishment of the first school taught by Benjamin Alexander in 1800 to the present day. Among their institutions are or have been: Campbell Academy, Brevard College, Abby Institute, Carroll Academy, Corona, Greenwood Seminary, Cumberland University, and Castle Heights School.

Revolutionary soldiers who settled in Wilson County were: James Scott, Jeremiah McWhirter, Anthony Gann, Philip Shackler, John Harpole, John Dabney, Edward Mitchell, and John Wynn.

Wilson County sent two companies to the War of 1812 under the command of Capt. John Hayes and Capt. Charles Wade, among whose soldiers were: Fred Askew, Joseph Settle, George Dillard, William Norman, William Hartsfield, Lawrence Sypert, Zachariah Tolliver, William Sypert, Kit Seaburn, James Carson, William Meyers, William Martin, Grief Randolph, T. K. Ramsey, John Shackleford, and William Harrison.

A company under Capt. J. J. Finley went from Wilson County to the Seminole War in 1836, and another company went in 1837 under Capt. W. L. S. Dearing. Among these troops were: T. J. Stratton, John D. Mottley, John Wilbury, P. Hern, J. N. Kennedy, Dawson Hancock, W. W. Talley, Nathan Oakley, George W. Lewis, E. S. Smith, Lewis Pendleton, William Watkins, J. H. Kennedy, Samuel T. Powers, and John Alexander.

Two companies also took part in the Mexican War under Captains Hayes and Smith.

Statistics of Wilson County: population, 1920, 26,241. Assessed valuation of taxable property, 1921, $21,653,882. Area, 536 square miles. Number of farms, 4,134. Railway mileage, 54. Drained by the Cumberland River and its tributaries. One of the best live stock counties in the state. Staple products are wheat, corn, oats, hay, tobacco, and live stock. Traversed by the N. C. & St. L. Railway and the Tennessee Central Railway. Lebanon, the county seat, is 30 miles from Nashville on the Tennessee Central Railway and has fine schools and churches. It is the seat of Cumberland University and Castle Heights Training School. Has two weekly newspapers, four banks, electric light plant, and manufacturing establishments, including a cotton and woolen mill, cannery, etc. Watertown is another prosperous town. Scholastic population of county, 9,277; high schools, 12; elementary schools, 107.

WEST TENNESSEE

BENTON COUNTY

BENTON COUNTY was erected on November 24, 1835, from parts of Humphreys and Henry Counties and was named in honor of Thomas H. Benton. It was organized on February 7, 1836, by the commissioners, Green Flowers, Ephraim Perkins, Lewis Brewer, John F. Johnson, and George Camp. They met at the house of Samuel Haliburton, in Tranquility, on the stage road from Nashville to Memphis, about a mile west of Camden.

The first settlement was made in 1819 by Willis and Dennis Rushing, on Rushing's Creek, about six miles north of Camden. Among the early settlers were: David Watson, Lewis Graham, Joseph Cowell, Zachary Barker, Benjamin Holland, Michael Fry, Cas Matlock, John Anderson, and James Wyly.

Camden, the county seat, was located on the land of John Jackson whose only title was that of occupancy. The town was surveyed and laid off in December, 1836. Irwin B. Carnes built the first dwelling in the town. Thomas H. Burton, Anderson Lashlee, and James Haywood also built about the same time.

The first courthouse was of logs, but in 1837 a two-story brick courthouse was constructed.

The officers of the first county court were: Thomas Haliburton, county court clerk; Thomas Jones, sheriff; John H. Williams, trustee; George Hollowell, county superintendent of schools.

The first newspaper published in the county was the Central Democrat, established by William Doherty in 1852. The first school in the county was started in 1822 or 1823 on Rushing's Creek. The teacher was Allen C. Presson. The first church, Primitive Baptist, was organized by George Turner and Levi Kirkland. Cowell's Chapel Church was organized in 1824 by Benjamin Peebles, a pioneer circuit rider and presiding elder of West Tennessee. Among the early Baptist ministers were: Obadiah Hardin, Jacob Browning, Lemuel Herrin, and Josiah Arnold. Early Presbyterian ministers were: Samuel T. Thomas, Abner Cooper, and H. Babbitt. Early circuit riders were: Thomas Smith, Robert Collins, and Levi B. Lee.

Statistics of Benton County: population, 1920, 12,045. Assessed valuation of taxable property, 1921, $5,207,788. Area, 412 square miles. Number of farms, 1,984. Railway mileage, 26. This county is bounded on the east by the Tennessee River. Portions of the county are well timbered. The surface is level and the soil generally fertile. This is one of the peanut-growing counties, and other staple products are corn, cotton, wheat, oats, vegetables, and live stock. Intersected by the N. C. & St. L. Railroad. Camden, the county seat, has a population of 800 and is on the N. C. & St. L. Railway. It has good schools, churches. a weekly newspaper, two banks, and flourishing mercantile establishments. Scholastic population of county, 4,332; high schools, 3; elementary schools, 62.

CARROLL COUNTY

ON October 19, 1818, Andrew Jackson and Isaac Shelby made a treaty with the Chickasaw Indians whereby all their lands east of the Mississippi River were ceded to the United States. Their lands within the limits of Tennessee became the Western District of this state and, on November 7, 1821, an act* was passed entitled, "An act to form and establish new counties west of the Tennessee River." Under the provisions of this act Carroll County was formed and named in honor of Gen. William Carroll, who was governor of the state at that time. It was organized on March 11, 1822, at the house of R. E. C. Dougherty, where the first court of Pleas and Quarter Sessions was held. Huntingdon, near the center of the county, was selected as the county seat, and the first session of the court was held there in a log courthouse on December 9, 1822.

The first settlers came from North Carolina, South Carolina, and Virginia, some locating as early as 1820.

This county furnished a company for the War with Mexico and several companies to each side in the War between the States.

Statistics of Carroll County: population, 1920, 24,361. Assessed valuation of taxable property, 1921, $12,243,353. Area, 600 square miles. Number of farms, 4,141. Railway mileage, 68. Drained by Big Sandy and Obion Rivers. Surface generally level, and there is considerable timber. Corn, cotton, wheat, fruits, and live stock are staple products. Fruit-growing and poultry raising are profitable industries. Huntingon,

---

*Chapter XXXII, Acts of 1821, page 39.

the county seat, has a population of 1,121, has good public and private schools, two newspapers, two banks, electric lights, water works, manufacturing establishments, and stores. McKenzie, another town, has a population of 1,630 and is on the N. C. & St. L. Railroad. It has fine schools, a weekly paper, churches, and prosperous business establishments. Truck-growing is one of the leading industries in Carroll County. Scholastic population, 8,331; high schools, 10; elementary schools, 90.

CHESTER COUNTY

CHESTER COUNTY was erected on March 1, 1879, from fractions of Madison, Henderson, McNairy, and Hardeman Counties and named in honor of Col. Robert I. Chester.* On March 19, 1875, a new county named Wisdom County had been erected out of the same fractions and this act was repealed by the act which created Chester County.

The early history of Chester County is the history of the counties out of which it was formed.

Statistics of Chester County: population, 1920, 9,669. Assessed valuation of taxable property, 1921, $3,998,171. Area, 288 square miles. Number of farms, 1,667. Railway mileage, 16. This county is on the high lands of West Tennessee and is drained by the Forked Deer River and intersected by the Mobile and Ohio Railroad. The soil is sandy and fertile. Cotton is the leading staple, but other crops are profitably grown. Henderson, the county seat, is on the M. & O. Railroad and has a population of 1,181. It has a weekly newspaper, good schools and churches, three banks, manufacturing establishments and stores. Scholastic population of county, 3,339; high schools, 2; elementary schools, 42.

CROCKETT COUNTY

CROCKETT COUNTY was erected on December 20, 1845, from parts of Haywood, Madison, Gibson, and Dyer Counties. The caption of the act is, "An act to establish Crockett County in honor of and to perpetuate the memory of David Crockett, one of Tennessee's distinguished sons." In this act commissioners were appointed to hold an election to ascertain if the voters in the fractions appropriated

---

*This distinguished man was quartermaster of the Fourth Tennessee Regiment, commanded by Col. Samuel Bayless, in the War of 1812.

to the new county acquiesced in this action. In 1846 Judge Read, of Madison County, decided that Crockett was not a constitutional county.

On July 7, 1870, the Legislature passed another act with the same caption as that of 1845, and this time Crockett County was constitutionally erected. In the latter act the commissioners appointed were: A. B. Howlett, James Emerson, David Whitacre, A. T. Fielder, G. W. Bettes, John Lyon, J. C. Thorp, and T. F. Conly. Considerable opposition from the old counties had to be overcome. E. B. Mason, of Madison County, filed injunction suits in the chancery courts of the four counties affected, but the organization of the new county was finally effected.

On March 9, 1872, an election was held for county and district officers; and the county court, with Isaac M. Johnson, chairman, was organized in the same month.

The circuit court was held on April 8, 1872, in Alamo, the county seat, named for the Alamo in Austin, Tex., where Crockett lost his life.

The earliest pioneers, about 1823, were: John B. Boykin, Robert Johnson, Giles Hawkins, Cornelius Bunch, John Bowers, E. Williams, and John Yancy.

Statistics of Crockett County: population, 1920, 17,438. Assessed valuation of taxable property, 1921, $9,235,694. Area, 275 square miles. Number of farms, 3,072. Railway mileage, 36. Drained by Forked Deer River and well timbered in parts. Soil in eastern portion sandy loam and clay and adapted to profitable growing of fruits and vegetables. Western portion is level and fertile and well adapted to the production of cotton, corn, wheat, and other staple crops. Alamo, the county seat, has a population of 720, has good schools and churches, two banks, flourishing stores, and manufacturing establishments. Bells, on the railroad, has a population of 920, good schools and churches, a weekly newspaper, two banks, manufacturing establishments and stores. Gadsden, Crockett Mills, and Maury City are other towns. Scholastic population, 6,037; high schools, 2; elementary schools, 47.

DECATUR COUNTY

DECATUR COUNTY was created in November, 1845, from a part of Perry County by Section 11, of Chapter VII, of the acts of that year. The wording is as follows: "That a new county be and is hereby established to be composed of all that part of Perry County lying on the west side of Tennessee River, to be known and distinguished by the name of Decatur County, in honor of and to perpetuate the memory of Commodore Stephen Decatur, of the United States Navy, of whose services our nation should be proud and whose memory should be revered."

The board of commissioners mentioned in this act to organize the county were: John C. Yarbrough, William J. Menzies, John S. Walker, Samuel Brashear, and David B. Funderburg.

The provision was also made that the act should go into effect "from and after the first Thursday in March, 1846."

Decaturville was chosen by popular election as the county seat.

Statistics of Decatur County: population, 1920, 10,198. Assessed valuation of taxable property, 1921, $3,182,916. Area, 310 quare miles. Number of farms, 1,813. Railway mileage, 11. Bounded on the east and south by the Tennessee River. Surface is comparatively level and covered with a fine growth of timber. Iron ore, marble, granite, and phosphate are found in the county. Corn, cotton, and hogs are staple products. Decaturville, the county seat, has a population of 315 and is five miles from the Tennessee River and the same distance from the N. C. & St. L. Railroad. It has good schools and churches, a weekly newspaper, a bank, and prosperous business establishments. Parsons, on the railroad, has a population of 429, good schools and churches, two banks, and prosperous business establishments. Scholastic population of county, 3,580; high schools, 4; elementary schools, 55.

DYER COUNTY

DYER COUNTY was erected on October 16, 1823, from the Western District and was named in honor of Col. Henry Dyer. It was organized in October, 1824, and, in accordance with a provision of the Court of Pleas and Quarter Sessions and of the circuit court, were held at the house of John Warren until 1826, when they were held in Dyersburg, the county seat. The magistrates of the first court were: John Rutherford, Benjamin Porter, John D. Burris, William Lyrrell, and Dr. Thomas Hash. The chairman was John Rutherford and the clerk William Mitchell.

The first settlement was made in 1820 at Key Corner, now in Lauderdale County. The second settlement, in 1821, was made about four miles east of Dyersburg by George Davis, William Martin, Jerry Pierce, and Willis Chamberlain. Dyersburg was laid off in 1825 and incorporated in 1826.

It is believed that the first house in the county was of logs and built by Elias Dement.

Statistics of Dyer County: population, 1920, 29,983. Assessed valuation of taxable property, 1921, $17,819,244. Area, 495 square miles. Number of farms, 3922. Railway mileage, 69. Bounded on the west by the Mississippi River and well drained by smaller streams. It is hilly, rolling, and level and is one of the most fertile counties in the state. Well adapted to the production of cereals, cotton, and other crops. Intersected by the Illinois Central Railroad and the Birmingham and Northwestern. Staple products are cotton, corn, wheat, potatoes, hay, lumber, and live stock. Dyersburg, the county seat, has a population of 6,444 and is a flourishing town, on both railroads, and 76 miles north of Memphis. It is a manufacturing town and has fine schools and churches, three banks, a weekly newspaper, and prosperous commercial establishments. Newbern has a population of 1,767, good schools and churches, a weekly newspaper, two banks, manufacturing, and commercial enterprises. Scholastic population of county, 10,769; high schools, 10; elementary schools, 75.

FAYETTE COUNTY

FAYETTE COUNTY was erected on September 29, 1824, from fractions of Hardeman and Shelby Counties and was named in honor of Marquis de la Fayette. As provided by the act, the sessions of the Court of Pleas and Quarter Sessions were held at the house of Robert G. Thornton, the first meeting being on December 6, 1824. The subsequent meetings of the court were held here until November, 1825. The chairman of the first court was Edmund D. Tarver, and the first clerk was Henry M. Johnson, who was the first settler of Somerville. Only one case was tried at the first session and brought into the treasury of the county six and one-fourth cents as a fine. Wolf scalps were taken as shown by the entries of the clerk. A tax of thirty-seven and one-half cents on one hundred acres brought in a revenue of $750, in 1825, in which year Robert Cotton was taxed on a four-wheel carriage, the only one in the county.

Settlements began about 1822, when Thomas J. Cocke, of North Carolina, located in the northwestern part of the county.

In February, 1825, the county seat, Somerville, was located on lands donated by George Bowers and James Brown, and the first session in this place was held in a log cabin on the public square. Three years later the first stage came to town.

Somerville was named in honor of Lieut. Robert Somerville, who was killed in the battle of Tohopeka.

Statistics of Fayette County: population, 1920, 31,499. Assessed valuation of taxable property, 1921, $13,974,350. Area, 630 square miles. Number of farms, 5,875. Railway mileage, 80. This county borders on the Mississippi River, and the surface is generally level and in portions well timbered. Cotton is the leading product in the county, but it is well adapted to fruits and berries, and this industry is developing. It is a large producer of strawberries. Cotton, corn, fruit, and live stock are staple products. Traversed by the L. & N., the Southern, and the N. C. & St. L. Railroads. Somerville, the county seat, has a population of 1,106 and is on the Loosahatchie River. It has fine schools and churches, a weekly newspaper, two banks, prosperous business establishments and is surrounded by fine cotton plantations. Scholastic population of county, 11, 771; high schools, 11; elementary schools 56.

GIBSON COUNTY

GIBSON COUNTY was erected on October 21, 1823, from the Western District, "in honor of and to perpetuate the memory of Col. John H. Gibson." The act provided that, at first, the courts should hold their sessions at the house of Luke Biggs, four miles from Trenton, which was called Gibsonport until 1825, when the court was held at Trenton for the first time.

The first magistrates commissioned were: William P. Leat, Robert Edmondson, Obey Blakemore, Benjamin White, Robert Read, — — Rice, Abner Burgan, John D. Love, William W. Craig, W. B. C. Killingsworth, John J. Lane, and F. Davis. The first session began on January 1, 1824, and William P. Leat was chairman and Thomas Fite, clerk.

The first settlement was made in 1819 by Thomas Fite and John Spencer, his brother-in-law. They came from Warren County and located about eight miles east of Trenton. David Crockett also lived in the same year near Rutherford and was joined in a few months by his family.

Early lawyers were: A. O. Totten, Felix Parker, and J. H. Talbot. Later lawyers were: John W. Crockett, who became attorney-general, John A. Talliferro, M. R. Hill, R. P. Caldwell, and Robila P. Raines. Gibson County has furnished three members of the State Supreme Court, viz: A. W. O. Totten, T. J. Freeman, and W. C. Caldwell.

Statistics of Gibson County: population, 1920, 43,388. Assessed valuation of taxable property, 1921, $26,048,985. Area, 615 square miles. Number of farms, 6,585. Railway mileage, 71. Drained by Obion and Forked Deer Rivers. One of the leading agricultural counties in the state. Surface generally level and very fertile. Portions are well timbered. Cotton is the leading product, and other staples are corn, wheat, fruits, vegetables, and live stock. Truck-growing is a leading industry, large quantities of early vegetables being shipped to northern markets. Trenton, the county seat, has a population of 2,751, and is on the Forked Deer River and the M. & O. Railroad. It has a number of manufacturing establishments, two weekly newspapers, good schools and churches, three banks, and prosperous mercantile establishments. Humboldt, at the junction of the M. & O. Railroad and L. & N. Railroad, has a population of 3,913 and is the center of a large trucking section. It has good schools and churches, a weekly newspaper, two banks, manufacturing and commercial establishments. It is a large shipping point for fruits and early vegetables, poultry and eggs. Milan, another town at the junction of the Illinois Central and the L. & N., has a population of 2,057 and is also a vegetable and fruit shipping point of importance. It has good schools and churches, a weekly newspaper, two banks, and manufacturing and commercial establishments. Scholastic population of county, 15,339; high schools, 30.

HARDEMAN COUNTY

HARDEMAN COUNTY was erected on October 16, 1823, from the Western District and was named in honor of Col. Thomas Jones Hardeman. By the act which created it this county was directed to have the first sessions of its courts held at the house of Thomas McNeil. On October 17, 1823, the county was organized by the following-named commissioners: Andrew Taylor, William Polk, Jacob Pirtle, John Y. Cochran, William P. Robertson, Nathan Stell, and John Rosson. William Polk was chosen chairman; Thomas Hardeman, clerk; J. C. N. Robertson, sheriff; of the first Court of Pleas and Quarter Sessions.

Settlements began in 1819, but the first notable settlement was made in 1821 by Col. Ezekiel Polk, grandfather of President James K. Polk; William Polk, son of Col. Ezekiel Polk; Thomas McNeal, son-in-law of Col. Ezekiel Polk; Thomas J. Hardeman and his grandson, Rufus P. Neely.

The committee appointed to select the county seat was composed of Abram Maury, William Hall, James Fentress and Benjamin Reynolds. They selected a site one mile north of the present location, and Maj. William Ramsey donated twenty-six acres for the site. The county seat was at first called Hatchie, but in 1824 the present site was selected and was called Bolivar in honor of Simon Bolivar, the patriot and liberator of Venezuela. Major Ramsey and Colonel Polk gave fifty acres for the new town site.

The first teacher in the county was, perhaps, Henry Thompson. Early papers were the Palladium, The Sentinel, and Free Press.

Bolivar is the home of the Western Hospital for the Insane.

Statistics of Hardeman County: population, 1920, 22,278. Assessed valuation of taxable property, 1921, $9,282,472. Area, 640 square miles. Number of farms, 3,535. Railway mileage, 95. Borders on the Mississippi River and is drained by the Big Hatchie. Its surface is nearly level and in sections covered with fine timber. Soil is fertile, and it is one of the best cotton producing counties. Other staples are corn and hay. Traversed by Illinois Central, Southern, and N. C. & St. L. Railroads. Bolivar, the county seat, is on the Illinois Central, 18 miles south of Jackson and has a population of 1,031, with good schools and churches, weekly newspaper, two banks, and manufacturing and commercial establishments. Scholastic population of county, 8,414; high schools, 6; elementary schools, 104.

HARDIN COUNTY

HARDIN COUNTY lies partly in Middle Tennessee and mostly in West Tennessee. It was formed on November 13, 1819, from the Western District and extended to the Mississippi River. It was named in honor of Col. Joseph Hardin. Colonel Hardin came from Roane County in 1815 with a grant for 2,000 acres of land for services as a colonel in the Revolutionary War. On the east bank of the Tennessee River, at Horse Creek, near Savannah, he located his land, settled there in 1818 or 1819 and established the nucleus for the county soon afterwards named for him.

His sons and daughters soon settled there, as did the Brazletons, Goodens, Thackers, Courtneys, Garners, Dicksons, Dorans, Duckworths, Cherrys, Kincannons, Sloans, Williamses, Boyds, Wisdoms, Rosses, Shannons, and others.

The first Court of Pleas and Quarter Sessions was organized in January, 1820, by the following-named magistrates: Isham Cherry, David Kincannon, James Barnes, Samuel Harbour, and Joseph McMahan. The first county officers were: Henry Mahar, ranger; Joseph McMahan, trustee; James Barnes, register; Stephen Roach, coroner.

The commissioners appointed for the purpose located the county seat in the approximate center of the county and called it Hardinsville, later known as Oldtown, where the county government functioned until 1830, when it was moved to Savannah, then called Rudd's Ferry, and a log courthouse was built. This courthouse was soon replaced by a brick structure.

The most outstanding event in the history of this county was the battle of Shiloh, or Pittsburg Landing, which was fought on the west bank of the Tennessee River on April 6 and 7, 1862. The National Cemetery is maintained at Pittsburg Landing and the Shiloh National Park, consisting of several thousand acres, in charge of DeLong Rice, is one of the most attractive and well-kept parks in the nation.

Statistics of Hardin County: population, 1920, 17,291. Assessed valuation of taxable property, 1921, $5,665,008. Area, 587 square miles. Number of farms, 2,907. Railway mileage, none. Borders on Alabama and Mississippi and intersected by Tennessee River, which is navigable the year round. Western portion generally level, while eastern portion is hilly, with fertile valleys. Eastern part well timbered. Staple products are cotton, corn, and live stock. Savannah, the county seat, is on the Tennessee River and has a population of 758, excellent schools and churches, a weekly newspaper, two banks, and prosperous mercantile establishments. Congress has established a national park at Shiloh, the scene of a battle during the Civil War. Scholastic population of county, 5,915; high schools, 6; elementary schools, 77.

HAYWOOD COUNTY

HAYWOOD COUNTY was erected on November 3, 1823, from the Western District and was named in honor of Judge John Haywood.

The first settler was Col. Richard Nixon who came from North Carolina in 1821. His grandson, Richard J. Nixon, was the first white child born in the county. Between 1821 and 1826 the following settled in the Nixon neighborhood: Gen. William Conner, Jesse Mauldin, John Saunderlin, and Nicholas T. Perkins. Colonel Nixon's father, a Revolutionary soldier, received for his services a grant of 3,600 acres in Haywood County. He located his home on Nixon Creek, four miles east of Brownsville.

Such was Nixon's prominence that his house is mentioned in the act creating the county as the place of meeting of the courts until provision otherwise should be made by law. Here, on March 8, 1824, was organized the first Court of Pleas and Quarter Sessions with the following magistrates in attendance: Richard Nixon, Clarence McGuire, Nicholas T. Perkins, Jonathan T. Jaycocks, Willie Dodd, B. H. Sanders, David Jeffries, and Blackman Coleman. Richard Nixon was elected chairman; B. H. Sanders, clerk; John G. Caruthers, sheriff; William H. Henderson, register; Richard Nixon, trustee; Jonathan T. Jaycocks, ranger; and Julius Sanders, coroner.

The commissioners "to select and set apart a site for the seat of justice" were: James Fentress, Benjamin Reynolds, and Robert Jetton. To them Thomas M. Johnson deeded fifty acres on December 14, 1824, for the county site, which was named Brownsville. The first courthouse, built in 1824-1825, was of logs and once imprisoned the notorious John A. Murrell, who escaped from it. It was succeeded by one of brick in 1845.

Statistics of Haywood County: population, 1920, 25,386. Assessed valuation of taxable property, 1921, $10,816,331. Area, 570 square miles. Number of farms, 4,359. Railway mileage, 29. Drained by the Hatchie and Forked Deer Rivers. Surface nearly level with an abundant supply of timber. Soil fertile and capable of great diversification of crops. Fruit growing is a profitable business. Staple products are cotton, corn, fruit, grass, and live stock. The L. & N. Railway passes through the county. Brownsville, the county seat, has a population of 3,062 and is on the L. & N. Railroad. It has good schools and churches, manufacturing establishments, a weekly newspaper, two banks, and is an important shipping point for cotton. Scholastic population of county, 9,332; high schools, 17; elementary schools, 76.

HENDERSON COUNTY

HENDERSON COUNTY was erected on November 7, 1821, from the Western District and named in honor of Col. James Henderson.

The earliest settler was Joseph Reel who, in 1818, located on Beech River, about five miles east of Lexington. Not long after this Abner Taylor located near the site of Lexington.

The first execution in the county was that of a slave woman who drowned the daughter of Dr. John A. Wilson.

Lexington was selected as the county seat in 1822 on land previously owned by Samuel Wilson.

Statistics of Henderson County: population, 1920, 18,436. Assessed valuation of taxable property, 1921, $6,561,186. Area, 530 square miles. Number of farms, 3,290. Railway mileage, 42. Drained by tributaries of the Tennessee River. Surface generally level and well timbered in some portions. Soil is fertile in valleys and river bottoms. Leading product is cotton, and other staples are corn, grass, and live stock. Lexington, the county seat, has a population of 1,792 and is on the N. C. & St. L. Railroad, which traverses the county. It has good schools, churches, two weekly newspapers, two banks, electric light plant, stave factory, and a number of prosperous stores. Scholastic population of county, 8,198; high schools, 1; elementary schools, 85.

HENRY COUNTY

HENRY COUNTY was erected on November 7, 1821, from the Western District and named in honor of Patrick Henry.

John B. House was the first settler in 1819. Other early settlers were: Joel and Willis Hagler, James Williams, William Wyatt, Rev. Benjamin Peoples, Rev. John Mauly, Abraham and William Walters, James Hicks, William Jones, Johannon Smith, Henry Wall, Reuben Bomar, William Porter, Thomas Grey, Jesse Paschal, James and R. D. Caldwell, Samuel Rogers, Adam Rome, Henry Humphreys, Lonis and Samuel McCorkle, Alex Harmon, Col. Richard Porter, Hugh W. Dunlap, John Brown, John Young, James and David D. Greer, and Dr. Jacob Brazwell.

The first session of the Court of Pleas and Quarter Sessions was held at the house of Peter Wall on the first Monday in December, 1821.

Paris was laid out early in 1823 by commissioners appointed by the Legislature on lands secured from Joseph Blythe and Peter Ruff. The first courthouse was built of logs.

The bench and bar of Henry County have included many distinguished men, among them being Joshua Haskell, William R. Harris, L. N. Hawkins, Jas. D. Porter, Andrew McCampbell, A. G. Hawkins, H. W. Dunlap, William Arnold, Isham G. Harris, Will C. Dunlap, Sol C. Brazwell, Edwin Fitzgerald, and Tom C. Rye. Other distinguished citizens are: John W. Crockett, eldest son of David Crockett, a member of Congress, 1837-1841; Howell E. Jackson, justice of the Supreme Court of the United States; John D. C. Atkins, Congressman of the United States in 1837, and also of the Confederate States and again, after the war, Congressman of the United State for five consecutive terms; Dr. E. W. Grove, the millionaire medicine manufacturer; Rev. Irl R. Hicks, the "storm prophet" of St. Louis; Porter Dunlap, State Treasurer, 1915-1919, and now a member of the State Utilities Commission.

Statistics of Henry County: population, 1920, 27,151. Assessed valuation of taxable property, 1921, $16,555,918. Area, 580 square miles. Number of farms, 4,286. Railway mileage, 60. County borders on Kentucky and is bounded on the east by the Tennessee River. Surface generally level and well timbered in some portions. Staple produces are cotton, corn, wheat, tobacco, peanuts, and oats. Well adapted to truck-growing, which is a profitable industry. Poultry business is profitable. Intersected by the L. &. N. and the N. C. & St. L. Railways. Paris, the county seat, has a population of 4,740. Fine public and private schools, good churches, two weekly newspapers, three banks, manufacturing establishments, and prosperous stores. Has electric light plant and water works. Other town are Henry, Springville, Puryear, and Whitlock. Scholastic population of county, 9,005; high schools, 10; elementary schools, 100.

LAKE COUNTY

LAKE COUNTY was erected on June 9, 1870, from a part of Obion County and named for Reelfoot Lake.

The earliest settlers in the county were probably Richard Meriwether, Robert Nolen, and Frank Longley, who located before 1825.

The first county court was held in Atheneum Hall in Tiptonville, which was chosen as the county seat on September 5, 1870.

The great outstanding feature of Lake County is Reelfoot Lake. This lake was formed during the earthquake convulsions of the winter of 1811-1812. It is about 18 miles long and from three-fourths of a mile to three miles in width. It is one of the most noted places in this country for fishing and hunting.

Statistics of Lake County: population, 1920, 9,075. Assessed valuation of taxable property, 1921, $7,779,841. Area, 210 square miles. Number of farms, 850. Railway mileage, 24. County is bordered on the north by Kentucky and lies between Reelfoot Lake and the Mississippi River. The county is well timbered. The soil is fertile, and staple products are cotton, corn, and hogs. Tiptonville, the county seat, is on the Mississippi River and has a population of about 1,000. It has good schools and churches, a weekly newspaper, two banks, and prosperous business establishments. Scholastic population of county, 3,728; high schools, 2; elementary schools, 25.

LAUDERDALE COUNTY

LAUDERDALE COUNTY was erected on November 24, 1835, from parts of Dyer, Tipton, and Haywood Counties, and was named "in honor of and to perpetuate the memory of Col. James Lauderdale, who fell at the battle of New Orleans on the night of December 23, 1814."

The first activities of white men looking to future settlements in what was ultimately to be Lauderdale County were exerted by Henry Rutherford in 1785. He located the famous "Key Corner" in that year and his surveys covered the famous part of Lauderdale, Crockett, and Haywood Counties. Although he and his brother John, sons of the famous Gen. Griffith Rutherford, both settled in this county at a later day, it is said that the first permanent settler was Benjamin Porter, who located in April, 1820, having brought his effects on a flatboat up the Forked Deer River. His son, Benjamin Porter, Jr., was the first white child born in the county.

Fulton, the oldest town in the county, was laid out in 1827 by James Trimble. Fulton was for some years a serious rival of Memphis.

The next oldest town, Durhamville, was established by Col. Thomas Durham in 1829.

The commissioners appointed to select the county seat named it Ripley, in honor of General Ripley of the War of 1812. On February 24, 1835, the commissioners, Howell Taylor, Nicholas T. Perkins, and David Hay, purchased from Thomas Brown 62½ acres on which the town of Ripley was laid out by Abel H. Pope. It is located about seven miles east of the center of the county. The first church was Turner's Chapel, established in 1829, near Durhamville, by Rev. William Taylor.

The first school was taught by Mrs. Edith Kinley at her home near Double Bridges.

The first newspaper was the Ripley Gazette, established about 1860 by Mr. Youngblood.

Statistics of Lauderdale County: population, 1920, 21,494. Assessed valuation of taxable property, 1921, $15,266,680. Area, 450 square miles. Number of farms, 3,406. Railway mileage, 26. Bounded on the west by the Mississippi River and drained by smaller streams. Surface nearly level, with a good growth of timber. Soil fertile, and the county is a large producer of cotton. Other staple products are corn, fruit, and live stock. The Illinois Central Railroad passes through the county. Ripley, the county seat, on the Illinois Central Railroad, has a population of 2,070. It has good schools and churches, a weekly newspaper, 4 banks, and manufacturing and commercial establishments. Henning and Halls are other towns in the county. Scholastic population of county, 9,587; high schools, 5; elementary schools, 68.

MADISON COUNTY

MADISON COUNTY was erected on November 7, 1821, from the Western District and was named in honor of President James Madison. The earliest settlers, however, arrived during the preceding two or three years. Among them were: James Cockrill, J. H. Regan, Adam Huntsman, James Brown, John T. Porter, Joseph Lynn, Robert H. Dyer, and Adam R. Alexander, the last named in charge of the Land

Office of the Tenth District. All these located in the vicinity of Jackson.

On December 17, 1821, the county was organized by the following named commissioners who constituted the first court of the county: Adam R. Alexander, Bartholomew G. Stewart, David Jarvett, William Atchison, Robert H. Dyer, John Thomas, Duncan McIvor, Joseph Lynn, James Trousdale, Herndon Harelson, William Braden, Samuel Taylor, and William Woolfork. Herndon Harelson was chosen chairman: Roderick McIvor, clerk; Thomas Shannon, sheriff; John T. Porter, register; James Brown, ranger; William Atchison, trustee; William Griffin, coroner; George White, John Fore, Elijah Jones, and William Doak, constables. Henry L. Gray, Alexander B. Bradford, and Robert Hughes qualified as attorneys.

The first courthouse was completed in September, 1822. Jackson, the county seat, named for Andrew Jackson, was located on the lands of Daniel Shannon, W. E. Butler, Joseph Phillips, and John McNairy. It was incorporated on December 16, 1845. Its first mayor was R. J. Hays; its first postmaster, Samuel Taylor; its first newspaper, the Gazette, founded on May 25, 1824, by Charles D. McLean, Elijah Bigelow and Ed Hays.

Early attorneys were: John Wyatt, Adam Huntsman, Milton Brown, Benjamin Gillispie, A. L. Martin, Stokely D. Hays, Micajah Bullock, J. S. Allen, Hugh W. Dunlap, Andrew McCampbell, and M. A. McKenzie.

The numerous mounds in Madison County indicate that this section was once the home of a populous community of prehistoric people.

The sale of lots in the town of Jackson began July 4, 1822, and lasted about one week. Joseph Lynn was allowed twenty dollars for whisky furnished at the sale to encourage bidding. The first purchasers of lots were George Todd, Herndon Harelson, Mark Fisher, Duncan McIver, William Broden, Wilson McClellan, James McKnight, Vincent Harelson, David Horton, J. H. Ball, Isaac Curry, William Espy, Alex. B. Bradford, W. L. Flaner, James Burress, James K. Polk, S. F. Gray, S. C. Crofton, Roderick McIver, and M. Leggett. James K. Polk bought three lots, costing the aggregate sum of $582.

Madison County furnished to the Seminole War of 1836 a company called The Grays, commanded by Capt. Jesse McMahon; also troops to the Mexican War.

Statistics of Madison County: population, 1920, 4,824. Assessed valuation of taxable property, 1921, $25,793,119. Area,

520 square miles. Number of farms, 4,467. Railway mileage, 115. Intersected by the Forked Deer River. Its surface is generally level. Soil very fertile, and staple products are cotton, corn, fruits, vegetables, and live stock. The Illinois Central, the Mobile and Ohio, and the N. C. & St. L. Railroads traverse the county. A large cotton mill is located at Bemis, near Jackson, employing a large number of operators. Jackson, the county seat, with a population of 18,860, is a flourishing city with the facilities of the three railroads named. It has large manufacturing interests and is a jobbing center for a large territory. Jackson has fine private and public schools and is noted as an educational center. It has daily and weekly newspapers and other large publishing interests. An artesian waterworks system owned by the city supplies the city with water. Scholastic population of county, 16,783; high schools, 14; elementary schools, 100.

McNAIRY COUNTY

McNAIRY COUNTY was erected on October 8, 1823, from a part of Hardin County and named in honor of John McNairy, whom President Washington had appointed one of the three judges of the Southwest Territory. The act creating this county directed that the first courts should be held at the house of Abel V. Maury, near the center of the county. At the first session of the court of Pleas and Quarter sessions held on the second Monday in January, 1824, a commission was appointed which selected for the county seat Purdy, named for John Purdy, a surveyor in the service of the government. Judge Joshua Haskell presided over this court which elected the following officials: Henry S. Wilson, sheriff; Joseph Barnett, clerk; Michael Cross, circuit court clerk; William Maury, register; Benjamin Rice, surveyor; Robert M. Owens, trustee.

The first white child born was Hugh Kerby, in 1821.

The first store was owned by John Chambers and Matt Griffith.

In 1855, the citizens of Purdy successfully resisted the efforts of the Mobile and Ohio Railroad Company to build their road through their town, which action caused a gradual decline in the place, so that when, in 1870, an effort was made to move the county seat to the railroad many favored the project. However, the effort was not crowned with success until 1890, when P. H. Thrasher gave the county a courthouse located at Selmer.

Strong characters of the early days were: Col. James Warren, Gen. John H. Meeks, William G. Jopling, John G. Gooch, and Maj. Benjamin Wright who fought in the battle of Tohopeka.

The first church organization in the county was Bethel, in 1828. This was a Presbyterian Church and was soon followed by the Baptist Church at Gravel Hill.

In 1857, Isaac Nash began in Purdy the publication of the West Tennessee Argus, the first paper published in the county. Two of the most eminent men whom this county has produced were John V. Wright and Col. D. M. Wisdom.

Statistics of McNairy County: population, 1920, 18,350. Assessed valuation of taxable property, 1921, $6,829,882. Area, 550 square miles. Number of farms, 3,263. Railway mileage, 42. Drained by the Hatchie River and affluents of the Tennessee. Part of the county is level, and in some portions of the county there is a fine growth of timber. Staple products are cotton, corn, and hogs. The Mobile and Ohio and the Southern Railway traverse the county. Selmer, the county seat, is on the M. & O. Railroad, 35 miles south of Jackson. It has good schools and churches, a weekly newspaper, 3 banks, prosperous business establishments, and a population of 546. Scholastic population of county, 6,127; high schools, 6; elementary schools, 109.

OBION COUNTY

OBION COUNTY was erected on October 24, 1823, from the Western District and named for the Obion River.

The first settler was Elisha Parker who located in 1819 in the northeast part of the county near the Weakley County line.

The first court in accordance with the act creating the county met at the house of William M. Wilson on January 19, 1824. This location was about three miles west of Troy, which was selected by the commissioners in 1825 as the county seat and which was laid out on land donated by William Polk.

The sessions of the court continued to be held at Wilson's home until the county courthouse was built at Troy in 1824.

Union City was laid out in 1854 on the land of Gen. G. W. Gibbs. It was incorporated in 1861, the first mayor having been Thomas Ray, and is now the county seat. One of the first resident attorneys was Charles McAlister. In 1842, S. W. Cochran, from Ohio, located in Troy and became one of the leading attorneys in that part of the state. Other early lawyers of Troy were: John C. Hawkins, J. W. Buford, T. C. Swanson, Thomas R. Shearon. Early lawyers of Union City were: D. D. Bell, Charles N. Gibbs, and William B. Gibbs.

Statistics of Obion County: population, 1920, 28,393. Assessed valuation of taxable property, 1921, $29,793,421. Area, 540 square miles. Number of farms, 3,378. Railway mileage, 73. This county is bordered on the north by Kentucky and on the west by Reelfoot Lake and is one of the richest agricultural counties in the state. Surface nearly level, and there is a plentiful supply of timber. The soil is rich and fertile, and staple products are cotton, corn, wheat, oats, and live stock. One of the best wheat-producing counties in the state. Intersected by the Illinois Central, the Mobile and Ohio, and the N. C. & St. L. Railroads. Union City, the county seat, has a population of 4,412 and is a flourishing town with fine schools and churches, various manufacturing establishments, up-to-date stores, two weekly newspapers, two banks, lumber mills, railroad shops, etc. Other towns are Kenton, Obion, and Troy. Scholastic population of county, 10,500; high schools, 11; elementary schools, 85.

SHELBY COUNTY

SHELBY COUNTY was erected on November 24, 1819, from Hardin County and named "in honor and to perpetuate the name of Isaac Shelby, late governor of Kentucky." A large part of the land now comprising the city of Memphis was originally granted by the State of North Carolina in 1783 to John Rice, who, in 1791, was killed by Indians while on a trading expedition in the vicinity of Clarksville. In 1794, Judge John Overton bought from Elisha Wright, the brother of John Wright, the five thousand acres of the Rice tract for five hundred dollars and, on the next day, transferred a half interest in it to Andrew Jackson, between whom and himself a beautiful and tender affection existed. Jackson, however, sold his interest before the property was developed. A part of his interest was conveyed to Gen. James Winchester, who named the prospective metropolis Memphis because of supposed resemblences to the ancient city of Memphis, Egypt.

Memphis was laid out by Judge Overton and incorporated in 1826 or 1827.

Marcus B. Winchester, a son of Gen. James Winchester, was the first mayor. Between him and Isaac Rawlings existed a bitter rivalry for many years. Rawlings had been a sutler with Jackson's army in 1813, and also an Indian agent. He was the first magistrate of Shelby County, holding the office without either election or appointment, but by common consent. He was a prominent and picturesque figure and succeeded Winchester as the second mayor of Memphis and was re-elected several times.

Keating, in his valuable "History of Memphis," says that no other American city was laid out on so generous a scale as was the case with Memphis according to the plans of Overton and Winchester; that every emergency in the life of a leading commercial point seemed to be provided for. It seemed to have everything except religious organizations, for there was not a church in Memphis until 1827, although it is believed that there were several within the boundaries of the county. The first religious services were held in the courthouse by Methodist circuit riders of whom the earliest was Elijah Coffee, who came in March, 1822, in a flatboat. A small meeting house was erected in the court square in 1826.

Keating says, "After the preacher came the press," referring to the fact that Phebus founded the first newspaper, called The Memphis Advocate. The first number appeared January 18, 1827.

In the early days of the existence of Memphis conditions were very rough. J. J. Rawlings said that when he went to Memphis in 1824 there was no such thing as society. "Nothing that deserved that name. There were a few boys or young men, adventurers, uncontrolled by any restrictions; no preachers, no ladies to visit; they ran riot as they pleased."

Whisky was twenty-five cents a gallon, and horse racing was the favorite past time.

In 1827 the county court was removed to Raleigh, which then became the county seat, a fact which aroused much indignation in Memphis. In that year an epidemic of dengue, or breakbone fever, broke out, followed next year by the first appearance of yellow fever. In 1828, also, South Memphis was organized as a separate municipality and for several years a rivalry between it and Fort Pickering, on the one hand, and Memphis on the other, was carried on with extreme bitterness. There was also keen rivalry between Memphis and Randolph. But, beginning with 1829, when stage coach service was established to Memphis as a center for important eastern points, the supremacy of that city was incontestable. The first railroad was the Memphis and LaGrange, begun in 1838 and never finished.

The first public road in Shelby County was ordered marked out by the county court in May, 1820.

The Nashoba Venture

Perhaps the first effort in Tennessee for the benefit of the many made by an individual, influenced by pure altruism, was inaugurated by Fanny Wright at "Nashoba," near Memphis, in 1825. With her own funds, alone, she bought a tract of 1,940 acres located on Wolf River, northeast of Memphis, and erected on it a school for Negroes whom she hoped to educate to prepare them for citizenship before setting them free. Strange as it may seem to many at the present day, she encountered little opposition and, on her list of trustees she had strong names, some even illustrious. They were: General La Fayette, William McClure, Robert Owen, Cadwallader D. Colden, Richardson Whitby, Robert Jennings, Robert Dale Owen, George Flowery, Camilla Wright, and James Richardson. She wished to give an object lesson in gradual emancipation. It was not at all that any instruction should inculcate the idea of social equality between the two races, nor did she have any sympathy with the professional abolitionists. She traveled over the South in the interest of her venture stating that her remedies for the evils of slavery were gradual emancipation and industrial education. Her school lasted several years. When she realized she would be compelled to abandon the project she chartered a vessel and herself accompanied her Negroes to Hayti where she set them free. The trustees, in 1831, restored the property to her.

Statistics of Shelby County: population, 1920, 223,216. Assessed valuation of taxable property, 1921, $273,256,558. Area, 728 square miles. Number of farms, 8,204. Railway mileage, 231. Bounded on the west by the Mississippi River, on the south by the Mississippi River, and intersected by the Loosahatchie and Wolf Rivers. Surface is level and portions well timbered. Soil is very rich and fertile, and one of the best cotton-producing counties. Staple products are cotton, corn, lumber, and hogs. Memphis, the county seat and the largest city in the state, has a population of 162,351. It is an important rail and river shipping point, being the largest inland cotton market in the country. Two fine bridges cross the Mississippi at Memphis. Has fine system of streets and sewers, and is supplied with water from a fine system of artesian wells. It is a large manufacturing point and is the jobbing center for a large territory, including states of the south and southwest. It is a large lumber market and also an important market for mules and horses. It is the center of the cotton seed oil industry in the South and the largest cotton seed oil market in the world. It is a rapidly growing city, and growing in importance as a manufacturing and distributing point. Has three daily newspapers and various other periodicals and large publishing interests, fine public and private schools, splendid banking facilities. The West Tennessee Normal is located at Memphis. Scholastic population of county, 68,654; high schools, 19; elementary schools, 141.

TIPTON COUNTY

TIPTON COUNTY was erected on October 29, 1823, from the Western District and named "in memory of Capt. Jacob Tipton, who fell at St. Clair's defeat." By the act which created this county provision was made that the county and circuit court should meet at the house of Nathan Hartfield, until otherwise provided for by law. Among the early pioneers were Gen. Jacob Tipton, son of Capt. Jacob Tipton, Dr. Hold, Captain Scurry, Major Lauderdale, George W. Frazier, K. H. Douglass, and Jesse Benton, brother of Senator Thomas H. Benton. Jesse Benton lived at Randolph and was very active in promoting the interests of that place which posed as a rival to Memphis, and which became a very important center of trade for all the western section except the counties of Shelby and Fayette.

Covington was selected as the county seat, which was located on land donated by John C. McLemore and Tyree Rhodes. In 1852 an effort was made to remove the county seat from Covington to Randolph, but it failed by a small vote.

Statistics of Tipton County: population, 1920, 30,258. Assessed valuation of taxable property, 1921, $15,074,391. Area, 400 square miles. Number of farms, 5,271. Railway mileage, 27. Bounded on the west by the Mississippi River. The soil is fertile and surface level except for a range of hills near the river. Well timbered and watered by running streams and artesian wells. Cotton, corn, wheat, oats, fruits, vegetables, and live stock are staple products. Traversed by the L. & N. and the Illinois Central Railroads. Covington, the county seat, has a population of 3,410 and has fine churches and schools, a weekly newspaper, three banks, electric light plant and water works, cotton mill, cottonseed oil mill and other manufacturing enterprises, and is a flourishing town. Brighton, Atoka, and Tipton are other towns. Scholastic population of county, 10,703; high schools, 11; elementary schools, 78.

WEAKLEY COUNTY

WEAKLEY COUNTY was erected on October 21, 1823, from the Western District and was named in honor of Col. Robert Weakley, one of the most prominent men of the early pioneers of Middle Tennessee, a member of Tennessee's first Legislature and Speaker of the State Senate in 1823.

Provision was made in the act which created this county that the sessions of this county and circuit courts should be held at the house of John Tyrrell until otherwise provided for by law.

The first settlers were: Reuben Edmonston and John Bradshaw, brothers-in-law, who located on Mud Creek in 1819. Alexander Paschal arrived in 1822 and was considered well-to-do, as his wife had seven dresses. The first cabin was built by John Bradshaw. The county was organized in 1825 and Dresden was selected as the county seat and laid out in that same year. The first courthouse was completed in 1827 and the first session of the court held in it in 1828. Prior to this time some of the sessions of the court had been held in the house of Benjamin Bondurant in Dresden.

Early members of the bar were: A. G. Bondurant, Henry A. Semple, John A. Garner, S. A. Warner, and John Grundy, son of Felix Grundy. Emerson Etheridge, the famous orator, was a resident of Dresden.

Early physicians were: Drs. T. C. Edwards, Joseph Irby, and Jubilee Rogers.

Early preachers were: Thomas Ross, Gilliland Holland, and Lorenzo D. Overall.

Weakley County furnished eleven companies to the Confederate Army and four companies to the Federal Army.

Martin was established in 1873 and incorporated in 1874.

Statistics of Weakley County: population, 1920, 31,053. Assessed valuation of taxable property, 1921, $21,969,965. Area, 620 square miles. Number of farms, 5,050. Railway mileage, 51. Drained by the Obion River. The surface is generally level and the soil fertile. Staple products are cotton, tobacco, corn, wheat, oats, fruits, vegetables, and live stock. The N. C. & St. L. Railway and the Illinois Central Railway traverse the county. Dresden, the count seat, has a population of 1,007, good schools and churches, lumber mills, stave factory, tannery, a weekly newspaper, three banks, and is a flourishing town. Martin, another prosperous town at the junction of the railroad, has a population of 2,837, good schools and churches, manufacturing establishments, prosperous stores, a weekly newspaper, and three banks. Scholastic population of county, 10,914; high schools, 15; elementary schools, 91.